Henry G.G. Grey

Ireland, the Causes of Its Present Condition,

and the measures proposed for its improvement

Henry G.G. Grey

Ireland, the Causes of Its Present Condition,
and the measures proposed for its improvement

ISBN/EAN: 9783337322731

Printed in Europe, USA, Canada, Australia, Japan

Cover: Foto ©ninafisch / pixelio.de

More available books at **www.hansebooks.com**

IREL

TH

CAUSES OF ITS PRE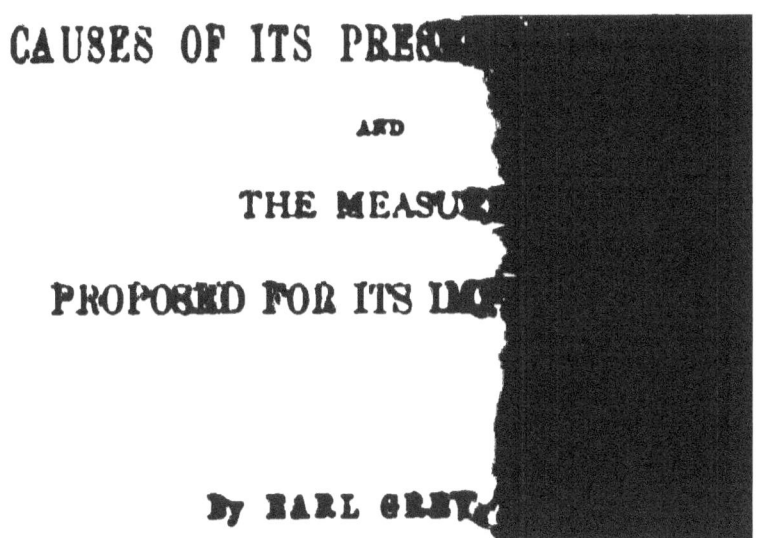

AND

THE MEASU

PROPOSED FOR ITS I

By EARL GR

LONDON:
JOHN MURRAY, ALBEMARLE
1888.

CONTENTS.

CHAPTER I.

PRELIMINARY OBSERVATIONS.

Long Discussions on Home Rule Project leave some Considerations bearing upon it requiring Further Notice—No Cause now to dread the carrying of the Project—Measures of a Dangerous Tendency to be feared from desire to conciliate its Advocates—Necessity admitted of Measures to Improve the Condition of Ireland—Caution required in Deciding upon them—The Present Evils result from Past Mistakes—These ought, therefore, to be Considered—No Advantage in looking back too far, and wrong to re-kindle Old Animosities—Enough to inquire what Errors have been Committed since the Union, and what are the Conclusions to be drawn from them as to Future Measures—Apology for Undertaking this Task . . . . page 1

CHAPTER II.

PARLIAMENTARY PROCEEDINGS RESPECTING IRELAND, 1800–1868.

First Mistake that the Act of Union was not followed by Measures for Removing the Disabilities of the Roman Catholics and making some Public Provision for their Clergy as desired by Mr. Pitt—Evils that arose from this—Controversy as to Emancipation—Sir R. Peel's Statement as to weakness of the

Government up to 1829 owing to its being Divided on this Question—Relief Act of 1829—Effect of its Long Delay—The Responsibility for this of Sir R. Peel and of his Colleagues—How Ireland has suffered from undue concern of Statesmen for Party Interests—Oppression inflicted on Irish Peasants by the mode of levying Tithes—No serious attempt to relieve them before the Tithe War of 1831-32—Remedy of the grievance delayed by question raised as to the Established Church—Party Contest on this Subject—History of bringing forward the Appropriation Clause, and its Abandonment—Failure of this Attempt to Conciliate the Roman Catholics unfortunate for the Nation—Remarks on the Conduct of both Parties on this Subject—For Thirty Years no proposal respecting the Irish Church submitted to Parliament by any Government—Debates in the House of Commons in 1843 and 1844—Opinions expressed in 1844 by Lord John Russell, Sir James Graham, and Sir R. Peel—Opinions expressed in Private by Men of all Parties contrasted with their Public Conduct—Interval of comparative Calm till 1868 . . . page 7

CHAPTER III.

CHANGE OF POLICY TOWARDS IRELAND IN 1868.—THE CHURCH.

Mr. Gladstone's Assault on Mr. Disraeli's Government on the Subject of Ireland in 1868—The First Step in it his Speech on Mr. Maguire's Motion in the House of Commons on the 10th of March 1868—Debate on that Motion—Speeches of Lord Mayo, of Mr. Chichester Fortescue, and Mr. Gladstone—Lord Mayo's Hints as to a possible Settlement of Church Question—Mr. Gladstone's Denunciation of "Dilatory Pleas" of the Government on this Subject, and his announcement of an Intended Motion upon it—Subsequent Defeat of the Government in the House of Commons and in the General Election that followed

—Complete Party Triumph, but Disaster to the Nation—Mr. Gladstone's Conduct—Mr. Disraeli's Opinion of his Policy; Mr. Gladstone's assertion that no part of the Church Property ought to be used for the Religious Instruction of the Irish People—Reason in favour of Public Provision for Religious Instruction of the People—Mr. Gladstone's Conduct; its effect was to overturn a rival Minister and to obtain Power for himself—His Accession to Power—Passing of Disestablishment Act of 1869—Prediction of Good to follow from it—Opposite Result—Change for the worse in the Condition of Ireland between 1868 and 1870—Mr. Gladstone's Statement of this change Exaggerated, but in the main True—Not Surprising—Impolicy of the Measure, and still worse effect of Language used in supporting it . . . page 36

CHAPTER IV.

IRISH LAND ACTS OF 1870 AND 1881.

The Land Law of Ireland required Amendment when the Bill of 1870 was brought forward—The Law then in Force had worked Badly—A Bill to Amend it brought into the House of Lords by Lord Clanricarde in 1867 referred to Select Committee, Amended, and recommended to the House—This Bill, with a Supplemental one, would have Redressed the Real Grievances of Irish Tenants—Bill proposed by Mr. Gladstone on an Opposite Principle—Contrast between the Two Measures—Injustice inflicted on Landowners by the Last—Measure Defended by Mr. Gladstone on the ground of the "Hunger for Land" of the Irish People —The "Hunger" Real, but caused by Insufficiency of Available Land—Possible Remedies—The Act of 1870 had an Opposite Tendency—Principle of the Act unsound, and its Practical Operation more Injurious owing to Circumstances of Ireland—Improvement of Agriculture its most pressing Want

—It was going on chiefly by exertions of Landowners, and against the Opposition of the Tenants—Experience of Mr. Bence Jones, Mr. Mahoney, and others—In the worst parts of Ireland improvement of Cultivation not practicable—Misery of the Population—Dr. Arnold's Account of their state Sixty-five Years ago—Uselessness of attempts since to give Temporary Relief—Mischievous Operation of the Act of 1870—Worst consequences of Measure—Encouragement of Lawlessness, and Demoralisation of Population by creating an appetite for Spoliation—Act of 1881, a new Measure of Confiscation against the Landlords, and a reward of the Violence and Outrages of the Tenants in 1880—Cry raised for Abolition of Landlordism—Mr. Parnell's object in raising it—Success of his Policy—Mr. Gladstone played into his hands—The Coercion Act of 1881 objectionable—The Land Act, its Faults, and those of the Policy, shown by the result—Comparison of the state of Ireland in 1863 and 1835—Lamentable Change, for which Mr. Gladstone is mainly Responsible—His Speech in Wales last June, describing the Condition of Ireland as "Intolerable," and the Fruit of Misgovernment, how far true; facts that ought to be considered as bearing on Mr. Gladstone's present Position on Irish Question—What that Position is—He promised good from Home Rule, but refuses to explain what Home Rule is—The failure of his former Promises ought to be a warning against trusting to those he now makes . . . . page 85

CHAPTER V.

WHAT MEASURES ARE REQUIRED FOR IRELAND.

Apology for the Proposals I shall make—Practice of taking Popular Wishes as the Guide of Legislation should be Aban-

CONTENTS.

denied—The Present Ministers seem instinct disposed to follow the Examples of Mr. Gladstone—The Land Act of 1887 another step in the same direction as the Acts of 1870 and 1881—Bad Results of former Land Acts a reason against further Legislation on the same Principles; and the Constitution generally owes to—Disposition to accept wild Schemes—One much in favour to enable Tenants to buy the Land they hold—Objections to the Money difficulty—Impolicy of getting rid of Landlords; probable effect on the state of Society of their Removal—Evils from the present relations of Owners and Occupiers of Land produced by unwise Legislation and inefficient Administration during many years; to cure them must be a work of time—Difficulty to be expected in enforcing fresh Contentions and enforcing Payment of Rents—Pressure will be brought to bear on Ministers—Importance of resisting it, and Reasons for doing so—By degrees a better state of things may be arrived at if there is no further unsound Legislation, and Order and Security are established—How Emigration may be useful—Some Opponents of Mr. Parnell's Scheme in favour of giving increased Powers of Local Self-Government to Irish people—These Powers they already have—Reasons against going further and creating either a single Council for all Ireland or one for each Province—Only one of the Powers Parliament exercises with regard to Ireland which it could with advantage—What is called the "Private Business" of Parliament relating to Ireland, ought to be done in Dublin rather than at Westminster—"Private" Legislation, both for Ireland and Great Britain, now conducted very ill—Reasons why a Reform is wanted, and Sketch of a mode of Effecting it—The Creation of any New Representative Body in Ireland would be useless for this purpose, and objectionable—The Manner in which Ireland has been Governed not to be approved—It has suffered much from Party Spirit in this Country—Evil much aggravated of late—Ireland has been Demoralised by what has happened, and its state now Deplorable—Two things necessary for a Change for the Better; firm Enforcement of the Law, and some arrangement to secure wiser Legislation—First, the most Important ; General Poverty of the Population at the bottom of Irish Discontent—Poverty owing to want of security—This security Ireland has never enjoyed—Lawlessness has more or less prevailed from the absence of proper firmness and energy in the Executive Government—Errors and Omissions in Legislation have contributed to impede Improvement—In the present state of the House of Commons, little hope that either of the requisites for the Better Government of the Country can be obtained—Grave question thus forced upon us: Can Ireland be rescued from the Evils it is suffering from without suspending there for a time the Operation of Representative Government? No such Proposal would at present be listened to; but the requisites for the Improvement of Ireland are now unattainable—Great Britain is also Suffering—These Evils are becoming Unbearable; the Country may soon have to choose between Surrender to the Home Rule Party and Depriving it of the Power it Abuses—The First not to be thought of—If the Nation should be convinced of the necessity of a Complete Change in the System of the Irish Government, there would be no difficulty in effecting it—Sketch of a Plan for this—Better Modes of accomplishing the object are, no doubt, to be found, but the object one it is necessary to attain—Some Measure not less strong than that described indispensable . . . . . . page 146

CHAPTER I.

PRELIMINARY OBSERVATIONS.

Since the time when Mr. Gladstone declared his intention of supporting Mr. Parnell's demand of "Home Rule" for Ireland, the subject has been so fully discussed in a multitude of speeches and publications that it is not unreasonably regarded as well nigh exhausted. There still, however, remain some considerations bearing upon it, which do not seem to me to have yet received as much notice as they deserve, and to which I am induced to solicit the attention of the public by the deep interest I have long taken in the welfare of Ireland, by my sense of the terrible evils that unfortunate country is now enduring, and by my fear that measures may be taken which will tend rather to aggravate than to cure these evils, and would also be likely to prove disastrous, not only to Ireland, but to the whole United Kingdom. In expressing my fear as to the measures which may be adopted, I do not mean that I have any apprehension that "Home Rule," as it is understood by Mr. Gladstone and Mr. Parnell, will be accepted by Parliament; the defeat of Mr. Gladstone's Bill of last year, and the emphatic approval given to its rejection by the nation in the general election, have relieved the country from that danger, not only for the moment, but, as I trust, for a long time to come. The protracted debates in Parliament and the public discussions during the Recess on the rejected scheme have done much towards convincing the British people that the union which binds England, Scotland, and Ireland, into one nation could not be dissolved without great injury to them all; and also that even the complete separation of Ireland from Great Britain, with all the evils it would infallibly produce, would probably do less harm to England than the attempt to maintain a nominal union with Ireland under such conditions as would exist if any scheme like that suggested by Mr. Gladstone were to be adopted. At length it seems to have become generally understood that it is necessary for the welfare of all the three divisions of the United Kingdom that they should continue to form a single nation, under the rule of a single authority, able to use their collective power and resources in support of their common interests. I have, therefore, little apprehension that the country will be brought to give its sanction to the scheme of Mr. Parnell and of Mr. Gladstone for destroying the union of Great Britain and Ireland, but I cannot shut my eyes to the fact that among those who earnestly desire to maintain that union there are many who contend for the adoption of measures of very dangerous tendency, for the purpose of conciliating the Irish supporters of Home Rule.

In what I have just said I am far from intending to deny either that we are bound to do whatever may be possible in order to conciliate the Irish people to the Imperial Government, or that the present state of Ireland affords sufficient proof of its having been heretofore misgoverned, and of the need there is for a change of system. No man can feel more strongly than myself how much requires to be done in order to raise Ireland from its present terrible condition, and how heavy a responsibility will rest upon England if any practicable means of effecting that object are neglected. But whilst it is clear that very decided measures are necessary for the purpose of correcting the evils by which Ireland is afflicted, we must not forget that many of these evils are of long standing, and owe their present intensity (as I shall endeavour to prove) to ill-directed attempts to abate them, and to unwise legislation. Great caution is therefore required in determining what ought now to be done; and, in order to arrive at a right conclusion, we ought carefully to inquire to what causes, and to what errors on the part of its rulers, the present unhappy state of Ireland is to be attributed. I do not mean that we ought to investigate the remoter causes of the various social ills with which Ireland is afflicted. It is true that these ills are not unconnected with errors and crimes of distant dates, for the history of the relations between England and Ireland during several centuries is a deplorable one. In the long struggle between the English and the Irish races in Ireland great faults were committed by both, and each was guilty of grievous wrongs to the other, which had their fruit in much suffering to both parties, and in evils of which abundant traces remain to the present day. But no good could arise from endeavouring to ascertain what share of blame fairly attaches to either party for long past misdeeds; on the contrary, all who have contributed to embitter existing controversies by reviving the memory of acts of cruelty and oppression committed by each party against the other, deserve the severest censure; and, unfortunately, by far the worst offender in this respect is to be found in a statesman, who has held the office of First Minister of the Crown, and still retains a high position in the country.

To guide our judgment as to the measures that ought now to be adopted with respect to Ireland, there is no occasion for looking back farther than to the beginning of the present century. By the union which was then accomplished, the Imperial Government and Parliament became far more directly responsible than they had ever been before for the administration of Irish affairs, and it is to the mistakes which have been committed since the passing of Mr. Pitt's great measure that we must mainly attribute the present unhappy condition of Ireland. I will endeavour to explain what, according to my judgment, these mistakes have been, and also what conclusions I think we should draw from their results as to the policy it would be right to follow in the time to come; and in order to make my views more intelligible, I shall not scruple to repeat (sometimes in the same words as before) statements I have formerly made, and arguments I have used both in Parliament and elsewhere.* I am well aware that the task I am undertaking is one to which I am far from being equal, and which it may perhaps be presumptuous in me to attempt, but I cannot resist my desire to do what little I can towards throwing light on the momentous question now before the country; and I venture to hope that the observations I shall offer may not be altogether useless, but may suggest matter for consideration to persons better able to deal with the subject than myself.

* I refer chiefly to speeches made in the House of Commons in the years from 1835 to 1838, and afterwards in 1843 and 1844, and in the House of Lords in 1846 and 1866; also to three articles in the "Nineteenth Century" of June 1882, and of September and November 1883.

CHAPTER II.

PARLIAMENTARY PROCEEDINGS RESPECTING IRELAND, 1800-1868.

IN considering what mistakes have been committed in the government of Ireland since the Union, the first that calls for remark is that which was made by passing the Act of Union, without its being followed immediately by the measures which its author regarded as necessary to complete it. It is well known that Mr. Pitt was of opinion that the grant of Catholic Emancipation, and the making of some public provision for the Roman Catholic priesthood, ought to have taken place as soon as the Union was accomplished. He was well aware that real contentment with the institutions of the nation could never exist in Ireland, so long as all who adhered to the form of Christianity professed by the great majority of its inhabitants were on that account excluded from Parliament, and from holding the higher posts in the public service. He also believed—and in my opinion justly—that the entire dependence of the Roman Catholic Clergy on their flocks exercised a pernicious influence both on the priesthood and on those to whom they ministered. Unhappily the bigotry of George III., and of the great majority of his subjects in England and Scotland, as well as of the Irish Protestants, made it exceedingly difficult for Mr. Pitt to relieve the Roman Catholics from the disabilities of which they justly complained; and though the king would have willingly concurred in making some provision for the priesthood, the Roman Catholics, both clergy and laity, very rightly refused to agree to any arrangement of this kind, so long as those who held their religion were denied the same political rights that their fellow-subjects enjoyed.

By resigning office when he found that his measure for the union of Ireland with Great Britain would not be completed by the grant of Roman Catholic Emancipation, Mr. Pitt relieved himself from blame for the great mistake thus committed. But whether he was justified in resuming his post at the head of the government on the fall of the Addington administration, without the power of making the concession he thought the Roman Catholics were entitled to, is a different question, on which there is room for doubt. There were not wanting reasons, which were at least plausible, for his yielding on this point to the determination of the king; but, on the other hand, his doing so had unfortunate consequences for the country that ought to have been foreseen. The controversy which raged on this subject up to the year 1829, and its effects in embittering the old animosities between Roman Catholics and Protestants, must be regarded as one of the chief causes of Ireland having failed to attain to a condition of internal tranquillity and prosperity. The prolonged struggle on the question of Roman Catholic Emancipation was in various ways an obstacle to the improvement of the country; the natural discontent of the Roman Catholics, with its necessary consequence of continued political agitation, greatly discouraged all kinds of industrial enterprise, and, as Sir R. Peel complained in 1829,* the Irish Government, during

* See his speech on the Address at the opening of the Session.

the years this struggle lasted, had been almost paralyzed by being divided on the great question of the day, the Lord-Lieutenant and his Chief Secretary sometimes taking opposite sides upon it, and, at others, the Lord-Lieutenant being at variance with the Secretary of State for the Home Department, under whom he had to act. With a government thus weakened by its internal division, as well as by the violence of the conflicting parties in the country, little could be done towards correcting the many faults to be found in the laws and social organization of Ireland. And, unfortunately, when at length the struggle was brought to an end by the passing of the Roman Catholic Relief Bill in 1829, the long delay of this act of justice, and the manner in which it was carried, prevented it from producing the good it ought to have done.

Its effects would have been very different had it been carried only four years earlier, when the House of Commons passed by a small majority a Roman Catholic Relief Bill, which was lost in the House of Lords, and when it was also prepared to make some public provision for the Roman Catholic clergy. The celebrated election for the county of Clare, with O'Connell's triumphant return (which the law could not prevent, though it did not allow him to take his seat in the House of Commons), had not then taken place, nor yet the stormy proceedings in Ireland under his lead which ensued, and caused the tardy concession of 1829 to be regarded as not having been made from a sense of justice, but as having been extorted by intimidation. This was the first time that the efficacy of intimidation in winning concessions from the Imperial Parliament was practically shown to the people of Ireland, and a heavy responsibility for teaching them a lesson so fruitful of evil rests upon those statesmen, who did not in 1825 use the influence they possessed to enforce the immediate passing of a measure, which it was obvious must be carried before long. This responsibility rests more especially on Sir R. Peel. From his own subsequent declarations, it is clear * that he had at that time become aware that the claims of the Roman Catholics could not be permanently resisted with success, and he could hardly have failed likewise to perceive that if these claims must ultimately be granted, they

* See the discussions on this point in the House of Commons on the 15th and 19th of June 1846, Hansard, 3 Series, Vol. LXXXVII.

ought to be so at once, since the only effect of delay would be to prolong a struggle, which was inflicting extreme injury upon Ireland, and much also on the rest of the United Kingdom. The power of enforcing the immediate settlement of the question by granting the claims of the Roman Catholics was also in his hands, had he chosen to use it, since in the then state of public affairs it was certain that no administration, which would not undertake to effect this settlement, could be carried on without his aid. If, therefore, when Sir F. Burdett's Emancipation Bill of 1825 had been carried through the House of Commons, Sir R. Peel had signified to Lord Liverpool his determination to retire from the government unless it would consent to use all its authority in order to secure the passing of the measure by the Lords, the Prime Minister must either have agreed to this with the assent of a sufficient number of his colleagues, or the administration must have been broken up, and another must have been formed to give effect to the policy of concession.

The main responsibility for the unhappy results that followed from delaying the grant of Catholic Emancipation at that critical time must consequently rest with Sir R. Peel, though some share of it must also fall upon the other Anti-Catholic members of Lord Liverpool's Cabinet, and especially upon the Prime Minister himself. Nor were those of the Ministers who voted in Parliament for Emancipation, and supported it by their speeches, exempted by so doing from their full share of responsibility, since by continuing in an administration which practically opposed concession, they rendered it possible for a government with this policy to be carried on. In fairness to Sir R. Peel, it is right to add that, while it is impossible to justify his conduct, when we consider it with the light thrown upon it by subsequent events, which have shown how much it would have been for the public good, and how much of evil would have been averted if he had taken the different course I have indicated as having been open to him, still we ought to remember that he could not have done so without very painful consequences to himself, and that he was in an exceedingly difficult position. There is no reason to doubt that he had sincerely believed for many years, and still continued to believe in 1825, that the admission of Roman Catholics to equal political power with Protestants was in itself inexpedient and dangerous, and he might therefore be naturally unwilling to promote it, even when he had become aware that the demand for this change of policy had grown too strong to be much longer resisted. He had probably also reason to think that Lord Liverpool, and some of his other colleagues, could not have been induced to join in using the influence of the government for the purpose of prevailing upon the House of Lords to accept the Emancipation Bill sent up to it by the House of Commons; his insisting upon this course being taken might therefore be expected to break up the administration, and not the administration only, but also the party with which he had been connected during the whole of his political life. No Popery feelings were at that time nearly as strong in England and in Scotland and among the Irish Protestants as they had been found to be in 1807, when they had been successfully made use of by Tory politicians to overthrow Lord Grenville's government and establish themselves in power, and it was still to Anti-Catholic support that this party owed much of the strength by which its ascendancy was maintained.

Hence it was certain that a Tory administration could not have proposed concession to the Roman Catholics without forfeiting the confidence of a large proportion of its most trusty adherents, so that if Lord Liverpool's government had been willing and able to carry the Emancipation Bill of 1825 through the House of Lords, so many of its supporters would thus have been alienated, as to leave it little chance of being long able to hold its position. What actually happened four years later shows that the fall of Lord Liverpool's administration, either at once, or in no long time, together with the disruption of the Tory party, would have been almost sure to follow from Sir R. Peel's declaring himself in favour of Roman Catholic Emancipation in 1825; it is not unreasonable, therefore, to believe that his not having done so may have been due, partly at least, to his reluctance to inflict so damaging a blow on his party.

If I am right in the conjecture I have just thrown out, it follows that the solicitude for the interests of his party felt by a distinguished statesman proved in this instance a great misfortune to the country; and this is a fact it is important to notice, because I am convinced that the chief cause of the many evils under which Ireland is now suffering is to be found in the sinister influence exercised by the desire of different political parties to promote their own party interest without sufficient regard for the interest of the public. In the history of Irish administration, both before, and since the union, there is abundant evidence of the baneful effects this sinister influence has produced. Party spirit we know has been the bane of free governments in all ages, and has proved a serious drawback to the many great advantages such governments possess over those of a different character; nor does there seem to be anywhere much prospect of its being got rid of. But general as it is, this evil seems, from various causes, to have been even more grievously felt in Ireland than elsewhere. When its union with Great Britain took place, the social condition of Ireland was so bad that there was most urgent need, both for better administration, and for wise legislation to correct the many and crying faults of the existing laws, in order to create a state of things more favourable to the improvement and welfare of the people. Unhappily this want has not been met, and if we look back at what has been done in the large part of this century which has now gone by, we find a sad record of unwise measures that have been adopted, and of good and needful ones that have been rejected, or delayed, or not proposed, because statesmen of all parties, in striving for political power, have deferred to the prejudices and mistaken wishes of those by whose aid it was most likely to be won or to be kept.

Errors of judgment may account for many mistakes in the government of Ireland, but not for all, or for the worst. For instance, it is well known to what intolerable oppression the Irish peasantry were subject from the levy of tithes under a law which needlessly aggravated the burthen of a payment, that must at any rate have been odious, as being required for the support of a church they regarded as heretical. Under this law tithes were levied directly from the small occupiers of land, in many cases in kind, and in a most vexatious manner, very commonly not by the tithe-owners themselves, but by lessees who had no scruple in straining their legal powers to the utmost in order to screw the last penny they could from the tithe-payers. Successive Lords Lieutenant of Ireland

and their Chief Secretaries cannot have been ignorant that the oppression thus inflicted on the occupiers of land had long been one of the chief causes of agrarian outrages, yet, for more than thirty years after the union, nothing was done for the effectual removal of so crying a grievance. Some petty improvements were made in the law relating to the levy of tithes, but it was only when the "tithe war" (as it was not unfairly called) assumed a serious aspect in 1831 and 1832 that any attempt was made to sweep away a system which was essentially vicious. This can hardly be accounted for except by supposing that, during the many previous years in which power had been held by the Tory party almost without interruption, the Ministers of the Crown were deterred from dealing decidedly with an evil which called so strongly for a remedy, because they were aware that such powerful interests in Ireland would be opposed to any real reform in this matter, that, by attempting to effect one, they must incur a serious loss of Parliamentary support. This appears to be the most probable explanation of its having been so long before any real effort was made to relieve the Irish peasants from the grievance they undeniably suffered from the mode in which tithes were levied. And, after the necessity for granting this relief had been generally recognised, it was still further delayed by a party struggle which arose on the question as to whether any part of the income derived from tithes in Ireland should be diverted from the support of the Established Church to purposes beneficial to the whole population.

What occurred on the question thus raised as to the Established Church affords a striking example of the evils that have been produced by the influence of party interests in Irish affairs. No one now denies that the position held by the Established Church in Ireland afforded just ground for complaint to the great majority of the people, yet I am not aware that it was ever distinctly asserted in Parliament that it was a grievance that ought to be redressed till after the meeting of the first reformed Parliament in 1833. During the long debates on the question of Roman Catholic Emancipation, it was generally contended by its supporters that its being granted would tend not to endanger, but to give increased stability to, the Protestant Church, as then by law established, which, in their opinion, might require to be reformed, but ought to be firmly maintained as one of our most valuable institutions. This line of argument was taken by almost all the ablest advocates of emancipation, and it is by no means clear that they were wrong, for there are no slight grounds for believing that in the first years of the present century the maintenance of the Protestant Church Establishment in the position it had so long held was not generally regarded as a serious grievance by the Roman Catholics, but would have been submitted to by them with little difficulty if they had been relieved from civil and political disabilities on account of their religion. If, in granting them this relief, the oppressive system of levying tithes had also been got rid of, and some public provision had been made for the Roman Catholic clergy, in accordance with the views of Mr. Pitt, it is in the highest degree probable that this arrangement would have been accepted as satisfactory. But the argument, that the disabilities of the Roman Catholics ought not to be removed because the Protestant Establishment would be thus endangered, could not be insisted upon (as it was) during several years by the opponents of emancipation, without creating a bitter feeling against the Establishment in those who were on this ground refused what they believed to be their right, and without also suggesting to their minds the inquiry whether, admitting it to be true that danger to the Protestant Establishment would arise from giving relief to the Roman Catholics, this afforded any just grounds for refusing it. And this inquiry naturally led to the further question whether it was right or consistent with justice to the Roman Catholic population of Ireland that the Protestant Church Establishment should be upheld in the exclusive possession of the large revenue devoted to religious purposes.

Accordingly, after the Roman Catholic disabilities had been abolished, and the struggle for parliamentary reform was over, the question was raised whether some part at least of the large income of the Protestant Establishment ought not to be withdrawn from it, and applied to some other purpose, so as to benefit the whole, instead of only a minority of the population. A decided majority of the first reformed House of Commons believed that this question was rightly raised, and that the Established Church of Ireland ought to be required to surrender a moderate amount of the property it held for objects of general utility. Few of those who held this opinion would have approved of more than a small deduction from what was considered the unnecessary wealth of the Church; fewer still had any clear idea how any money taken from the Church could be employed for the benefit of the Irish people, and all admitted that, in any measure that might be adopted, vested interests ought to be respected, and that no clergyman ought to be deprived of the income he actually held. Still, though their opinions as to what ought to be done were very vague and very conflicting, a considerable majority of the members of the House of Commons of 1833 had a strong sense of the injustice of maintaining the Protestant Established Church of Ireland in the position it held, and an earnest desire that this injustice should be corrected. This desire was not satisfied by the act passed in 1833 for the reform of the Irish Church. This measure, it was asserted, did nothing towards meeting the just claims of Roman Catholic population of Ireland, and the necessity for one of a different character continued to be pressed on the attention of Parliament. In the new House of Commons elected after Parliament had been dissolved in the last weeks of 1834, the members who took this view of the subject were less numerous than they had been in the former one, but those who adhered to it more or less decidedly were still a majority, though a small one, of the house. And the question soon became that on which parties were divided; the refusal of Sir R. Peel to make any concession upon this subject arrayed against him several members of the House of Commons, who would not otherwise have joined in opposing him, with the result of bringing about the fall of his administration, and the formation of Lord Melbourne's.

The new administration lost no time in asking Parliament to give its sanction to the policy its members had contended for when opposing Sir R. Peel. The question whether this policy should be adopted was raised by bringing into the House of Commons a bill for the commutation of Irish tithes, containing a clause which provided that, in certain cases, a portion of the revenue derived from tithes should be applied to purposes of general utility instead of to the support of the Protestant Church. No deduction of this kind was to be made from the income of the Church in such a manner as to prevent its real wants from being sufficiently provided for, and the whole amount it would have had to give up would have been so small as to be really insignificant. The clause for this purpose, which was known as the "appropriation clause," was opposed with much determination, and though it was carried in the two successive sessions of 1835 and 1836 by small majorities in the House of Commons, it was rejected by very large ones in the House of Lords. In 1837 the progress of a third bill was stopped by the early dissolution of Parliament in consequence of the death of the King. In 1838 it was found that the attempt to collect tithes under the existing law was doing so much injury in Ireland that it could hardly be continued. It was also clear that it was impossible to carry through the House of Lords any bill for the commutation of tithes, if it contained the obnoxious appropriation clause which had met with little support in the country; the government therefore determined to abandon this clause, and brought in and passed a tithe commutation bill not containing it. There can be little doubt that this was the right course to take, though, after what had occurred in the last three years, it necessarily exposed the government to reproaches, for which there were at least plausible grounds. The boon which had been asked for the Irish people was so small in itself that, even if it had been carried in the first instance, it would have had little value, except as showing a kindly feeling towards them on the part of the government and of Parliament. The hope that it might be so accepted had vanished in the bitter struggle it had caused, and it would have been idle to continue this struggle for the sake of the much contested, but really insignificant, appropriation clause.

This failure of an attempt to conciliate the Roman Catholics of Ireland by making some concession to them on the subject of the Established Church proved very unfortunate for the nation, and looking back, at this distance of time, to the course of the struggle, it must, I think, be confessed that neither of the great parties in the state came out of it with credit. If, in 1835, and the following years, the Conservatives, instead of offering a determined resistance (in which Mr. Gladstone took a leading part) to even the slightest diminution of the property held by the Protestant Establishment, had shown a disposition to concur in some very moderate concession to what are now generally recognised as having been fair claims put forward for the Roman Catholics, it is almost certain that the latter might then have been brought to acquiesce in an arrangement which would have proved very advantageous for all parties. On the other hand, the Whig leaders of that time made what I thought then, and I think still, was the great mistake of reducing their demands on behalf of the great body of the Irish people so low as to deprive themselves of all really strong grounds for insisting upon a change. In the debates on the appropriation clause it was painfully evident how little there was to be said for it except as a protest against the existing state of things. Among those who took an active part in supporting the clause, there must have been others, by whom this must have been as strongly felt, as it certainly was by myself. We had powerful (and as I think unanswerable) arguments to urge against maintaining the Church as it was, but all these arguments went to show the necessity not of such a measure as was, proposed, but of some far larger one, a fact which, for my own part, I never attempted to hide. But if, as I believe, Lord Melbourne's administration made a mistake in not asking for a larger concession to the just claims of the Irish people, it must in fairness be admitted that reasons of much apparent weight were not wanting for the course that was taken. The proposal of a larger measure which would have done more justice to the Roman Catholics would have had no chance of success without the support of the Conservative leaders, which was not to be looked for. In the then state of opinion such a measure would have been as unpopular in England and in Scotland as Catholic emancipation had been at the beginning of the century, and bringing it forward must, in all probability, have led to the fall of the administration. The Roman Catholic leaders in the House of Commons were aware of this, and naturally were not anxious that an attempt should be made to legislate in their favour, when it was likely to have no other result than the transfer of the authority and patronage of the executive government from hands they regarded as friendly to them, to others which they considered the reverse. It was with their acquiescence, therefore, that the petty concession they would have obtained by the appropriation clause was recommended to Parliament by Lord Melbourne's administration, instead of a really statesmanlike measure for the settlement of the Irish Church question. Still I am of opinion that the decision which was come to was wrong, and that in the face of almost certain failure a good measure ought to have been proposed. I am convinced that this would in the end have proved far more for the benefit of the nation than acting in a manner, which for a long series of years placed the advocates of religious equality in a false position.

During the thirty years that followed the abandonment of the appropriation clause in 1838, no proposal was submitted to Parliament by the government, whether in the hands of one party or the other, for dealing with the question of the Irish Church, nor did even Liberal administrations give any countenance to the attempts which were made from time to time by independent members of both Houses to obtain a recognition of the injustice and impolicy of maintaining that Church in its actual condition. So late as 1866, a Liberal administration (in which Mr. Gladstone held the important post of leader in the House of Commons) resisted in both houses motions having for their object to relieve the Roman Catholics of Ireland from the wrong done to them by allowing the Protestants to continue in the exclusive enjoyment of the large property which had been devoted in ancient (and much of it in Roman Catholic) times to the religious instruction of the nation. Yet, in the many years that this grievance was thus suffered to remain without any serious effort being made for its redress, it was well known to the leading statesmen of all parties that its existence was one of the main obstacles to every kind of improvement in Ireland, and one of the chief causes of the political disaffection which prevailed there. The truth of this assertion is placed beyond all doubt by the speeches made in Parliament on various occasions, and more especially in the two remarkable debates on the state of Ireland in the House of Commons in the years 1843 and 1844.

In the first of these years, the subject was brought under discussion by Mr. W. Smith O'Brien, and in the next by Lord John Russell, who moved for a committee of the whole house on the state of Ireland. Both debates were continued by adjournments for many days, the last for no fewer than nine, and in both a large part of the speeches which were made was devoted to the Church question. In these speeches, whether made from one side of the house or the other, it was generally admitted that the state of Ireland was highly unsatisfactory, and that the position held by the Protestant Established Church was at least one of the main causes of its being so. In 1844, when the subject was brought under consideration by Lord John Russell, as leader of the opposition, this opinion was not only strongly expressed by him and by those who supported his motion, but it was also hardly less distinctly avowed by the ministers. Sir James Graham, the Secretary of State for the Home Department, admitted that "with respect to the people of Ireland, the most important of all subjects which could be considered was the Protestant Church by law established," and said he was "afraid it lay at the bottom of all their difficulties with respect to the government of that country." Sir R. Peel, the Prime Minister, after describing how much his administration had effected for the good of the nation, added these remarkable words: "But at the same time we cannot but confess that with this—*intestinum et domesticum malum*—this unfortunate condition of Ireland we cannot look upon the picture with unmingled satisfaction." In speaking of this "unfortunate condition of Ireland," he did not attempt to deny its connexion with the Church question, or to prove that the Roman Catholics had not a real grievance to complain of. He rather laboured to point out objections to all the various plans which had been suggested for redressing or mitigating this grievance than to defend the principle of maintaining the Church of a small minority of the richest of the population in the possession of a large endowment, while the clergy of the great majority, and of the poorest of the Irish, were left to depend solely on the contributions of their flocks. Such a mode of dealing with the question leads almost irresistibly to the conclusion that, while Sir R. Peel would not venture to propose a change, he felt that the maintenance of the Protestant Church of Ireland, in the position it then held, could not be successfully defended on the grounds either of justice or good policy. But he had, at least, this excuse for not attempting to redress a grievance of which he scarcely denied either the existence or the evil effects, that the leader of the opposition had avowed that he was no more prepared than himself to make such an attempt. Sir R. Peel could point out that, although Lord J. Russell had described in very strong language the wrong done to the Irish people by the existing state of things, he had expressly declared that for the present at least no one of the different measures he had suggested for putting an end to this wrong was practicable. Sir Robert said, with truth, that in Lord J. Russell's speech there was "nothing whatever that could compel him when in office to adopt any course different from that of the present government."

From the remarkable debate I have been referring to, it appears that, although in 1844 one of the great parties in the state strongly asserted that upholding the Protestant establishment in Ireland was unjust and impolitic, and this was so faintly denied by the other as almost to amount to an admission that the assertion was true, yet the leaders on both sides equally shrank from submitting to Parliament any distinct scheme for the redress of a grievance they knew to be working very great evil to the nation. By so acting, it cannot be denied that they incurred a heavy responsibility, and for upwards of twenty years longer they persevered in the same course, nor is there any difficulty in finding at least a probable explanation for their having done so. In the great party struggle on the appropriation clause in Lord Melbourne's administration, the old "No Popery" feeling had been so strongly manifested both in England and in Scotland, that it was clear much unpopularity and loss of influence must be risked by any government or party that should venture to ask Parliament to adopt a measure for doing justice to the Roman Catholics of Ireland in respect of the Church establishment. An unwillingness to incur this risk, and thereby to give an advantage to rivals in the contest for power, must be regarded as having probably been the reason why both the great political parties in the state so long avoided making any serious effort to remove this cause of Irish discontent. This is the more to be believed, because during the years in question a large proportion of the men of soundest judgment and of most experience in political affairs of all parties did not scruple, in private conversation, to avow their opinion that what would be most for the public good, and be the best and fairest mode of settling the question, would be to make some moderate provision for the Roman Catholic clergy out of the property of the establishment, though the avowal was generally accompanied by an expression of regret that such a measure was impracticable. No doubt it was so, but only because among those who conducted the affairs of the country there was not sufficient concern for the public good to make them put aside their differences, and join, without regard to party interests, in calling upon the nation to adopt what they must have felt in their hearts to be the right course. If the leaders on both sides had joined in explaining to the English and Scottish people the good policy, as well as the justice, of making the concession I have described to the Irish Roman Catholics, I have no doubt that, in spite of the narrow and intolerant spirit which prevailed among too many of our countrymen, a measure might have been passed, which would have removed one of the principal causes of disaffection in Ireland. Unfortunately, no such appeal was made to the good sense and feelings of the people, and the conduct of both the great Parliamentary parties on this subject continued to bear the marks of being guided by party objects and party interests, instead of by a wise consideration of what was good for the nation. I do not consider it necessary for my present purpose to support this assertion, by an examination of the mode in which Ireland was governed, and of the proceedings in Parliament during a period of more than twenty years after the debates in 1843 and 1844 to which I have referred. It is sufficient to remark that, after a comparative calm, which lasted till 1868, the affairs of Ireland in that year again became the subject of a fierce party conflict, which ended in a complete change in the policy of the government and of Parliament towards that part of the United Kingdom. The manner in which this change was brought about, the character of the new policy that was adopted, and its effects, I propose to consider in the next chapter.

CHAPTER III.

CHANGE OF POLICY TOWARDS IRELAND IN 1868. THE CHURCH.

IN considering the nature and effects of the change in the nation's policy towards Ireland brought about by Mr. Gladstone's defeat of Mr. Disraeli's Government in 1868, it is necessary to bear in mind how the great party struggle that led to this result was raised, and what was the state of Ireland when it began. Mr. Gladstone's speech, on the motion made by Mr. Maguire in the House of Commons on the 10th of March 1868, for a Committee of the whole House on the state of Ireland, must be regarded as the first move in the assault upon Mr. Disraeli's administration, which was to end in its fall, and in the accession to power of Mr. Gladstone and his followers. In this speech, which was soon followed by more

decided action, he indicated that he had selected
the Irish Church question as the ground for an
attack on the existing government. The speeches
(some of them exceedingly able) made in a
debate that lasted through four nights, by other
members of various parties and opinions, supply
valuable materials for forming a judgment as to
what was then the real condition of Ireland, and
as to what justification was to be found in it for
the line of conduct taken by the leader of the
Opposition.

Looking first to what was said as to the state of
Ireland at that time, it is to be observed that,
although those who took part in the debate
differed widely from each other in their views as
to the manner in which the government of the
country had been conducted in past times, and in
which it ought to be so in the time to come, there
was comparatively little difference among them
with regard to the most important facts bearing
upon the actual condition of Ireland. None of
the speakers on either side of the House asserted
that condition to be satisfactory, but, on the other
hand, no one seriously impugned the truth of
the assertion made by Lord Mayo (then Chief

Secretary to the Lord Lieutenant), in a very interesting and statesmanlike speech, that this condition was an improving one; and many of the statements he made in support of his assertion were expressly confirmed, and even added to by other speakers. Among other things it seemed to be generally admitted that, since the country had got over the crushing calamity of the potatoe disease and the famine it produced, there had been a marked diminution in the misery and wretchedness in which a large proportion of the Irish people had formerly lived, there had been a considerable advance in wages, and some improvement in agriculture, though the mode of cultivating the land was still too generally unskilful and improvident. Trade was increasing, and it was shown that the tonnage of merchant ships arriving and departing had in the last years increased faster in the Irish than in English ports. Some new branches of industry showed signs of taking root. The Fenian conspiracy had been successfully put down, having received little or no countenance from the occupiers of land; out of 1,100 persons who had been arrested for treasonable practices in connexion with that conspiracy, only twenty-four

having been really occupiers of land. There had
been a great diminution of agrarian crimes, and the
maintenance of order had been rendered much easier
than in former times, by the fairness with which
juries in criminal proceedings had discharged their
duties. On this all important point of the increased security in the country, what was said by
Lord Mayo received strong confirmation from the
Opposition side of the House. After expressing
his opinion that the Fenian conspiracy had been
of an exceedingly formidable character for this,
among other reasons, that it " numbered amongst
its leaders strangers, or semi-strangers, trained in
the dangerous school of civil war in another
country," Mr. Chichester Fortescue (now Lord
Carlingford) went on to say, " The true difference,
in the present instance, as compared with former
occasions of a similar kind in Ireland, was this:
that, while the revolutionary movement was more
formidable, the forces on the side of law and order
were much greater. Those forces now consisted,
not merely of the Protestant body, but of a very
large and influential class among the Catholics in
Ireland, who had grown enormously in wealth,
influence, and good feeling towards this country,

under the more just and salutary system of legislation pursued in recent years. That observation extended to the clergy, those connected with the land, the mercantile, professional, and almost the whole middle class. He appealed, as an illustration of this, to the admirable conduct of the Irish juries during the late political trials. They had performed their duty towards their country with true patriotism, and an independence worthy of all praise."*

Such was the testimony of Mr. Chichester Fortescue (who had not long before been Chief Secretary to the Lord Lieutenant under a Liberal government) as to the state of things in 1868, and it was supported by that of Mr. Gladstone. In the same debate, in accepting Lord Mayo's account of the improved condition of Ireland, he said, "I rejoice to hear of the progress that has been made in Ireland. I do not feel that, by admitting that progress in the largest terms, we in the slightest degree weaken—on the contrary, I believe we much enhance—the argument for taking those yet further steps which remain to complete the connection between the two coun-

* Hansard, vol. cxc., p. 1594.

tries. There is a diminution of the grievous
distress which so long ground down the masses of
the Irish population. I do not inquire into the
extent of that diminution, or how much of that
distress remains. I admit the diminution, and
rejoice at it. There is a change, if not more important, at least equally important, and that is
that, in the classes above the want of the immediate necessities of life, there has grown up within
the last generation a sentiment of attachment to
law and order greater, more substantial, more
lively, and more effectual, with a view to the
administration of justice, than has ever perhaps
been known in former times. A great achievement, and let me add, a yet greater encouragement."* A strong proof of the real improvement
that had within a few years taken place in the
condition of Ireland is to be found in a fact mentioned by Mr. Maguire, that land, which formerly
might have been had at fifteen, twelve, and even
ten, years' purchase, had since been selling at
twenty-five, twenty-six, and even twenty-seven,
years' purchase."† Mr. Maguire did not refer to
this fact as affording ground for satisfaction, but

* Vol. exc., p. 1745.   † Vol. exc., p. 1291.

seemingly rather the reverse; yet it affords the very best evidence that a sense of security (the indispensable foundation of national prosperity) had been wonderfully increased in Ireland.

But, while it was thus generally admitted that there had been a marked improvement in the material condition of Ireland, it was contended by members on the Opposition benches that there was so much discontent, and even disaffection, to the Imperial Government, in a large part of the Irish people as to give grounds for very serious apprehension. Nor was this altogether denied by the government speakers. They did not appear to consider the ill-feeling towards England as strong as it was represented to be by others who took part in the debate, still its existence was distinctly admitted, and it was further admitted by Lord Mayo that it was partly at least produced by the position held by the Established Protestant Church in the midst of a Roman Catholic population, and by faults in the state of the law on the relations between landlords and tenants. The most serious of these faults he said that the government hoped to correct by a bill which would immediately be brought in, but he added that the subject was one of so much difficulty and complexity that further enquiry was necessary before all the improvements in the law as to the tenure of land which would probably be required could be attempted. In making this announcement, he pointed out both the unsoundness of some of the popular ideas on this matter, and the danger of ill-considered legislation with regard to it. His language on this question was that of a wise and cautious Statesman, and it would indeed have been well for Ireland if its law of landlord and tenant had been dealt with in this spirit, instead of with the rashness, the contempt of recognized principles, and the instability of purpose, which were displayed in the mischievous Land Acts of 1870 and 1881; from how much irreparable evil would the nation have been saved, and how much suffering to all classes of its people would have been averted. But what I have to say on this subject must be postponed; the great party struggle which changed the nation's policy towards Ireland was taken upon the question of the Irish Church, and, before entering into other matters, I must call attention to the circumstances and results of that struggle.

I have already mentioned that the first move in it was made by Mr. Gladstone in the debate on Mr. Maguire's motion of the 10th of March. Lord Mayo on that occasion threw out some vague suggestions as to a possible settlement of the Irish Church. On these suggestions Mr. Gladstone put what seems a strained and inaccurate interpretation, and after condemning them with unsparing severity, he went on to declare that this question ought to be dealt with at once, and in a very different manner from that contemplated by Lord Mayo. He found fault with what he called the "dilatory pleas of Her Majesty's Government" with regard to the Church, and speaking for himself and his supporters, he said that what "we seek and desire must be an operation, which for Ireland shall finally and conclusively, as far as we are concerned, set aside and put out of view all salaried or stipendiary clergy." And he intimated that, unless Mr. Disraeli (who had not yet spoken) should make a statement as to the views of the government more satisfactory or rather entirely different from the declarations of his colleagues, it would be the duty of the Opposition to make a proposal, and ask "the opinion of the House upon the question of the Irish Church." This proposal "ought to be plain, simple, and intelligible, in its terms," and after some other remarks he added, "it ought to be a declaration attended with some step or proceeding, which will give to the people of this country, and to the people of Ireland, conclusive proof that we have not entered hastily or lightly upon a task of so much gravity; that we mean what we say, and that, so far as depends upon us, the task will be performed." From this language it was clear, and it became more so in the sequel, that Mr. Gladstone intended to use the Irish Church question for the overthrow of the existing government, and was resolved to reject, or to render hopeless, and so prevent, any attempt the Ministers of the Crown might be inclined to make to settle this difficult question by amicable arrangement and by compromise, instead of by a party contest. Acting apparently with this view, he advised Mr. Maguire to withdraw his motion, as one "upon which they ought not to take issue with Her Majesty's Government," in order that he might himself, by a motion in a different form, obtain from the House of Commons a clear declaration of its opinion on the question of the

Irish Church. The motion he shortly afterwards made for this purpose was one to which the government could not agree ; and, having been defeated upon it, and still more completely in the appeal made to the country by the dissolution of Parliament a little later, Mr. Disraeli's administration had to retire, and Mr. Gladstone succeeded to power, with the support of a large majority in the House of Commons. The party triumph was complete, but looking to its results, and to the strong grounds there are for believing that very opposite results might have been obtained if a different course had been taken by those who gained it, I am constrained to believe that the triumph to a party was a disaster to the nation, and that Mr. Gladstone, by seeking it as he did, proved himself to be wanting either in the foresight and judgment of a wise statesman, or in the sense of duty, and in the preference of public to private interests, which are indispensable to the character of an honest politician. To some of the considerations which have led me to this conclusion I must now solicit attention.

I have shown that the condition of Ireland in 1868 was admitted on all sides to be much improved from what it had been for many years, and to be still improving. Nothing had contributed more to bring about this improvement than the comparative tranquillity the country had lately enjoyed. It is true that agrarian disturbances had till very recently been prevalent in some districts, and that the Fenian conspiracy had been a cause for alarm, still the country had on the whole been more quiet than it usually had been. Since the House of Commons had overthrown the administration of Sir Robert Peel in 1846 by rejecting a bill for giving additional powers to the government of Ireland, no Irish question had furnished ground for a great parliamentary contest between political parties; and, since the collapse of the abortive insurrection of 1848, there had also been a decided lull in Ireland of the political agitation of former years. This freedom from political disturbance, although it was as yet imperfect, and had lasted too short a time for its endurance to be reckoned upon, was certainly one, and probably by far the most important, of the causes to which the improvement that had taken place in the welfare of the people of Ireland was due. To render this partial political calm more complete, and to avert the dangers that threatened its continuance, ought therefore, at the time I am speaking of, to have been the object of the true well-wishers of Ireland. For such dangers existed, and by far the most serious of them was that arising from the position of the Protestant Established Church, which it was manifest could not long continue unaltered.

What was especially to be dreaded was, that the change, which must soon come, might be accomplished in such a manner as again to fan into a blaze the smouldering fire of the evil passions of religious partizanship which in past times had done so much harm in Ireland. The circumstances of the time were, however, favourable for a well-directed attempt to guard against this danger by such a settlement of the difficult question of the Church as might tend, not to revive old animosities, but to create more friendly relations between those who had been hitherto so bitterly hostile to each other as adherents of rival Churches. Though the Roman Catholics of Ireland were showing a sense that was becoming stronger from day to day of the wrong done to them by upholding the Protestant establishment as it then was, and also of their own growing power, they had not as yet taken any steps which afforded grounds for supposing that they would not have listened to a proposal made in a conciliatory spirit for placing them, with regard to their religion, on a footing of equality with their Protestant countrymen. Plain signs were also to be observed that the Protestants on their side were no longer so unanimously or so determinedly hostile as they had been to any concession being made on this subject to their Roman Catholic fellow-subjects. No doubt, the great majority of the Protestants still retained the opinions of their fathers as to their right to the position they had so long held, and their devotion to the Orange party and to Protestant ascendancy, was still strong. But, while this was the feeling of the majority of Protestants especially in Ulster, even those who entertained it could not altogether resist the entrance into their minds of another, though perhaps a secret, feeling that the ground on which they stood was slipping away under their feet, and that their resistance to a change, of which the prospect was hateful to them, must in the end be fruitless. Their unacknowledged consciousness of weakness must have prepared even the Orangemen for surrender without violent opposition, if indulgence for their prejudices, and a regard for their legitimate interests, had been shown, in a measure proposed for the relief of the Roman Catholics from a grievance of which they had a right to complain. There were also a good many Protestants even in Ireland who would not merely have acquiesced in the passing of such a measure, but would have hailed it with satisfaction as right in itself. A similar feeling prevailed still more widely among English Protestants, and especially among men of education and intelligence accustomed to take a serious interest in public affairs. I have already mentioned that, more than twenty years before, there were many Conservative as well as Liberal members of the House of Commons who did not scruple in private to express their wish that a settlement of the question could be accomplished on the principle of compromise, though they were deterred from an open expression of their opinion by the power which the old "No Popery" cry was supposed still to retain over their constituents. Since the subject had been discussed in the House of Commons in 1844, the number of those who were more or less openly in favour of concession had increased both within and without the walls of Parliament, and it now included at least a few of the ablest and most enlightened of the clergy of the Established Church in Ireland as well as in England.

If, in this state of opinion, the timid hints in favour of a compromise thrown out by Lord Mayo, in his speech on Mr. Maguire's motion, had been met by Mr. Gladstone in a conciliatory spirit, instead of by a fierce denunciation of any attempt to delay, even for the shortest time, the adoption of an extreme measure for putting an end to the Church Establishment of Ireland, it is not impossible, nor even improbable, that an amicable settlement of the question might have been accomplished. I do not mean to say that Mr. Gladstone ought to have been satisfied with what had been said on behalf of the government, or that he was wrong in his determination to call upon the House of Commons to express a decided opinion in favour of giving speedy relief to the Roman Catholics of Ireland from a grievance of which they had a good right to complain. Nor have I any fault to find with him for having selected a motion for resolutions declaring this opinion as his mode of raising the question. There was ample justification for his taking this step, but I am convinced that, if in framing the resolutions he was to move, he had been guided by a sincere and single-minded concern for the public good, and by wisdom to discern what would most promote it, they would have been very different from those which he eventually carried. The first of these resolutions, following the line he had taken in his speech on Mr. Maguire's motion, declared " That the Church of Ireland should cease to exist as an establishment, due regard being had to all personal interests and to all rights of property." And in his speech explaining his motion, he said that what he meant to condemn was, that there should exist, "supported by the income of the state or by public or national property in any form, a salaried or stipendiary Church."

By adopting the resolution in this form, and explained as it was by its author, the House of Commons pledged itself not merely to relieve the Roman Catholics of Ireland from a grievance

of which they justly complained, but also to
accomplish this purpose by absolutely prohibi-
ting the application of national property in any
manner to the religious instruction of the Irish
people. I do not find that any reasons that were
even plausible were assigned for calling upon the
House of Commons to agree at that time to the
last part of this proposition. Admitting, as I do,
the urgent necessity there was for its declaring its
determination to give speedy redress in this
matter of the Church to the Irish Roman
Catholics, there was no advantage, but, on the
contrary, much evil, in thus hastily pledging the
House of Commons to any particular mode of
doing so. By Mr. Gladstone's own admission, no
important legislation as to the Church could possibly be attempted in the session then in progress,
and in a Parliament which must of necessity be
soon dissolved; and Mr. Gladstone himself, as Mr.
Gathorne Hardy (now Lord Cranbrook) had just
reminded him, had only three years before pointed
out to the House that the real question was what
would be the right remedy for existing evils, and
had then gone on to observe that, " we no sooner
come to look upon this question practically than

we light upon a whole nest of problems of the utmost political difficulty." * This assertion was no less true in 1868 than it had been in 1865, when it was made by Mr. Gladstone; there were still "problems of the utmost political difficulty" to be solved, before a sound judgment could be formed as to what would be the best mode of correcting an acknowledged evil, and it was contrary to the plainest rules of prudence to ask the House of Commons to decide at once in favour of one particular scheme for doing so, before there had been even an attempt to consider whether other and better schemes might not be suggested. Mr. Gladstone's purpose of securing redress for the grievances of Ireland would have been no less effectually attained than it was by the resolutions he proposed, if he had only asked the House to affirm that injustice was done to the great body of the Irish people by maintaining the Protestant Church of Ireland in the position it then held by law, and that this injustice ought to be corrected without delay. If he had proposed a resolution to this effect, and it had been assented to by the House of Commons, it would have been

* Hansard, vol. clxxviii, p. 431.

rendered impossible for any ministers to hold
office without dealing with the question, and its
early settlement, either by the existing or by some
other administration, would have been assured.

Nothing, therefore, would have been lost for the
public object of his proceeding, if Mr. Gladstone
had made his motion in the form I have mentioned, and much might have been gained. Possibly it might even have led to what would have
been of such inestimable benefit to the whole
United Kingdom, and more especially to Ireland—
the settlement of the difficult question of the
Irish Church without any fierce party contest.
This would have been accomplished if the leaders
of the two great political parties in the state
could have been induced to forget for a time the
petty interests of party for the sake of the high
interests of the nation, and would have joined in
an endeavour to bring about some arrangement
that would have been fair to all concerned.
Perhaps it was hardly to be hoped that so happy
a result could be attained, but there would have
been at least a chance of its being so, if the House
of Commons had been only asked to resolve that
redress ought to be granted to the Roman

Catholics of Ireland in the matter of the Church, leaving the mode of granting it open for future consideration. And this further, and by no means insignificant, advantage would have been gained, that a party contest on this exciting question must probably have been deferred till after the general election. It was brought on earlier by the defeat of the government in the House of Commons before the dissolution of Parliament in 1868, on Mr. Gladstone's resolutions for the disestablishment and disendowment of the Protestant Church in Ireland. But that defeat would not have been likely to occur if Mr. Gladstone had moved a resolution of a different character, since it could hardly then have been resisted by the government. So long before as in the debate on Lord J. Russell's motion respecting Ireland in 1844, Mr. Disraeli had stated very strongly his opinions, that upholding the Established Church in Ireland for the exclusive benefit of the small part of the population to which it could be of use was one of the main causes of Irish discontent, and that it ought to be removed by adopting the principle of "religious equality." This opinion Mr. Disraeli had never retracted, on the contrary, his speeches in 1868 distinctly implied his adherence to it; he could not, therefore, without manifest inconsistency, have opposed a resolution moved by Mr. Gladstone if it had been to the effect I have suggested, while there would have been powerful reasons for assenting to it. By resisting the resolution, Mr. Disraeli and his colleagues were sure to incur a parliamentary defeat, with little or no chance of getting this decision of the existing House of Commons reversed by a new one, so that the speedy fall of the administration was to be looked for. On the other hand, by assenting to the resolution, they would no doubt have given offence to no small number of their supporters, who showed themselves to be still under the dominion of the old "No Popery" feeling, but a large proportion of the Conservatives in the House of Commons would probably have approved of their decision, so that no immediate danger to the administration would have been likely to arise from hostility in their own ranks, and no intention of attacking them on other grounds had as yet been shown by the Opposition.

The administration might, therefore, be expected

to stand, at all events, till it met the new Parliament, to which it would have been bound to submit a measure for the settlement of the Irish Church question, but with an unfettered discretion to propose such an arrangement as it might consider to be most just to all concerned, and most likely to prove beneficial to the nation. The circumstances of the time were (as I have already remarked) rendered favourable for the successful execution of the task that would have been imposed on the ministers, by the change of opinion which had for many years been gradually taking place among Protestants as to the expediency of striving to maintain the Irish Established Church in the position it held, and likewise by the absence of any general hostility on the part of the Roman Catholics to the British government. There were also signs that the clergy of our own Church as a body would not have been found so ill-disposed, as they were generally believed to be, to consider favourably the question of making a great change in the position of the Established Church in Ireland. They would probably, with few exceptions, have thought it their duty to resist any proposal for stripping the Church of its whole pro-

perty, or even of so much of it that the funds
left at its disposal would not have enabled it
to provide by judicious and economical arrangements for the payment of reasonable stipends to a
sufficient number of clergymen for the due discharge of its duties. But with a strong feeling of
opposition to allowing the Church of Ireland to
be deprived of the means really necessary for
carrying on its proper work, there was joined, in
the minds of many of its clergy, a belief that its
success in this work, and its usefulness, would be
increased by its consenting to make even a large
sacrifice of its property, if by such a concession an
arrangement could be brought about to relieve it
from the charge that pressed so heavily upon it
of being unjustly kept up to the injury of the
population it was intended to serve. They could
not help being conscious that, among impartial and
intelligent observers from foreign countries, an
overwhelming majority regarded the maintenance
of the Protestant establishment in Ireland in the
position it then held as unjust to the great body of
the people who were devoted to the Roman
Catholic faith, nor could they refuse to admit it
to be true that an institution, which had for its

object to teach the sublime laws of Christian duty, could not be expected to prosper if its very existence violated these laws by injustice.

This view of the subject had of late years gained so many adherents, not only among the laity, but also among Protestant ecclesiastics of the highest character in England as well as in Ireland, that there was no probability of any strong opposition being offered on the part of the clergy to a just and reasonable proposal for reforming the Irish Church made in a conciliatory spirit, though such a proposal must have caused a loss to the Irish Church, not only of wealth, but also of its position as one of the great institutions of the state. No measure for the settlement of the question could have succeeded unless it included the grant to Irish Roman Catholics of that complete religious equality with the Protestants which Mr. Disraeli had contended for in 1844, and this equality could not exist so long as the Church of the minority of the people was the Church of the state. This position, therefore, the Protestant Church must cease to hold, and it would consequently have been necessary that an authority should have been created in the Church itself for the management of its affairs by some such arrangement as that which was adopted in the Disestablishment Act of 1869. The mode of constituting the authority might probably have admitted of improvement, but the principle must have been the same with that on which the Act afterwards passed was founded, and there is reason to believe that this would not have been objected to by the friends of the Church. The Roman Catholic Church would also have required an organization of the same kind, which might easily have been created by calling on the prelates of that Church, and some of its lay members who would have commanded the confidence of their countrymen, to point out in what manner they would desire that a council should be formed to undertake the duty of applying for the benefit of their Church any annual sum that might be placed at their disposal.

I know it has been said that the Roman Catholics of Ireland would not have accepted endowment from the State in any form whatever, and declarations to that effect, which had been made on their part, were quoted in the debates both of 1844 and 1868. But, if these declarations are carefully considered, it will be found that what they really indicate is a determination not to agree to any scheme by which the Roman Catholic clergy would have been made stipendiaries of the state. To this they would have been quite right to object; but their legitimate objection to a proposal of this kind would not have applied to one, by which a fixed annual sum would have been made payable by Act of Parliament to the Roman Catholic Church, to be applied for its benefit at the discretion of a council constituted as the members of the Church might think best. An income to be so held, and placed in such hands, might have been accepted by the Roman Catholics without any fear of injury to the independence of their Church, and with such manifest advantage for the performance of its duties that there would have been little chance of its being rejected. The Roman Catholic Church has never been indifferent to the advantage of having sufficient revenues at its command to provide for maintaining its clergy without leaving them entirely dependent on the voluntary contributions of their flocks; on the contrary, its priesthood has often been charged, and not altogether without reason, with having been too anxious to secure property for their Church, sometimes (as its enemies allege) by bequests obtained from dying sinners by questionable means. At this moment the Roman Catholic Church of Ireland is known to be in possession of considerable wealth derived from the gifts or bequests of its members. In 1868, when there were as yet no indications that either the Roman Catholic clergy or the peasantry of Ireland were under the dominion of the bitter hatred of the British Government and nation, since engendered in their minds by the unwise measures that have been taken in the hope of gaining their affections, there was no reason to despair that the Roman Catholics, as well as the Protestants of Ireland, might have been induced to acquiesce in a measure for the settlement of the Church question on the principle of religious equality, if it had been brought forward in a judicious and conciliatory manner. There would indeed have been serious, but not I believe insurmountable, difficulties to contend with in framing such a measure, and especially in finding resources sufficient to provide an income, even on the most moderate scale, for each of the three

Churches which would have had claims on the available funds. Though it would be idle now to discuss the subject, I believe that it would not have been impossible to get over this difficulty without seeking aid from the British Treasury, on which it would have been impossible to throw any charge for this purpose, and wrong if it had been possible.

Any other difficulties that were to be anticipated would have been less to be feared, and, on the whole, it seems probable that if Mr. Gladstone had been willing to co-operate with the ministers then in power, or if he had even abstained from using the question for their overthrow, Mr. Disraeli would have successfully attempted to settle the difficult and dangerous controversy as to the Irish Church by an equitable compromise. No such attempt was made; nor is this hard to be understood. A compromise was only practicable on the basis of making some contribution from the national resources of Ireland towards the support of the three Churches, which include among their members nearly the whole Irish population. But Mr. Gladstone had announced his intention of offering a determined resistance to all proposals for allowing public money to be used for the support of the clergy of any denomination, and in the debates which had taken place it had been shown that, with regard to any payment to the Roman Catholic Church, his resistance would have met with much support from members on the ministerial side of the House, who were still under the influence of the old feeling of hatred to "Popery." Mr. Disraeli and his colleagues might, therefore, not unnaturally think it inexpedient to recommend a measure of compromise (though it is to be inferred from the language of Lord Mayo, as well as of Mr. Disraeli himself, that this would have been in accordance with the opinion of both), when there appeared to be no chance of such a measure being carried against the opposition that was declared to it, and it could not have been proposed without alienating a considerable number of those whose support was important to their party. Whether it would not have been better, both for their party and for the nation, that they should have incurred defeat by boldly proposing a resolution laying the grounds for a good measure, instead of such an unmeaning amendment to Mr.

Gladstone's resolutions as that which was moved by Lord Stanley (now Lord Derby) on behalf of the government, is a question I will not discuss.

For the reasons I have just explained, I hold that the settlement of the question of the Irish Church by an amicable compromise would not have been impossible, if, in the year 1868, Mr. Gladstone had not insisted that no part of the property of the Established Church in Ireland should be used in contributing to the support of the clergy of any Church whether Protestant or Roman Catholic. He recognized the right of the existing holders of preferment in the Church at that time by law established to continue to receive during their lives the incomes they then enjoyed, but he absolutely refused to consent that anything whatever should be taken for the religious instruction of the people from the considerable amount of the property of the Church which would remain available after providing for existing interests. I affirm that neither justice nor the real good of the nation required that the rule thus laid down by Mr. Gladstone should be followed in dealing with the Irish Church, but that, on the contrary, much evil was to be expected from insisting upon it. The injustice complained of as being done to the Roman Catholic by maintaining the Protestant Church Establishment did not consist in devoting its large revenue to the religious instruction of the Irish people, but in applying the revenue to this, which was generally acknowledged to be its intended and legitimate purpose, in such a manner as to make it of use only to a small minority, chiefly of the richer classes, while the great majority and the poorest of the population derived no benefit from it whatever. This was a real grievance, but it would have been completely redressed without diverting the large income set apart for religious instruction to other purposes, by conceding to the Roman Catholics, and to the Presbyterians, fair shares of its amount, and at the same time a great boon would have been conferred upon the distressed inhabitants of the poorest districts of Ireland. It is well known that in these districts the necessity of providing entirely at their own cost for the support of as many priests as are necessary for the performance of the rites of their Church is a heavy burthen on the scanty resources of the Roman Catholic peasantry, and therefore if the authorities of the Roman Catholic Church had had a fund placed at their disposal from which they might have paid the whole or part of the stipends of the priests whose flocks were least able to maintain them, a very sensible relief would have been afforded to a part of the Irish population which stands most in need of assistance. And this would have been attended with the further and important advantage of rendering the faithful and fearless discharge of their duty by the priests less difficult than it must be while they are left absolutely dependent for their support on the contributions of their flocks.

By insisting that nothing should be taken from the property of the Established Church to assist in maintaining the clergy of any denomination, all these advantages were thrown away, and, with them, the means of accomplishing an indispensable change of policy without giving greater offence than could be avoided to the Protestants of Ireland. To a large proportion of their body this change was sure to be distasteful, but if it had been proposed that out of the valuable property, of which the whole had been enjoyed by the Established Church, a moderate annual payment should be assured to its members to assist them in carrying on its work by their own exertions when it was dis-established, and that a grant should also be made to the Presbyterians in lieu of the Regium Donum, the objections of many Protestants to the policy of establishing complete religious equality might have been removed or mitigated, and this would have been of the highest importance for the future welfare of Ireland. But the wisdom of showing as much consideration as possible for the feelings of the Irish Protestants in adopting a measure which was necessary to do justice to the Roman Catholics, seems not to have been understood by Mr. Gladstone and his followers, and the course they took justified the remark made upon it by Mr. Disraeli, who said in the debate on the 16th of March 1868, " In my opinion a policy in Ireland of conciliation, which is commenced by outraging the feelings and humiliating the pride of a million and a half of men most loyal, most intelligent, and very wealthy, is not a wise policy. It may be a party triumph, but it will not in my mind tend to the national welfare."* This anticipation, as I shall endeavour to show, has been but

* Hansard, Vol. cxc., p. 1791.

too completely verified; and no attempt has been made to show that the refusal to allow any part of the property held by the Established Church to be used for the religious instruction of the Irish people (which necessarily led to the policy condemned by Lord Beaconsfield) was required for the public good. Mr. Gladstone asserted that this refusal was indispensable, but I have not been able to find that he even explained upon what grounds it ought to be so regarded. It can hardly be that he holds it to be wrong in principle for a nation to sanction any public provision for instructing the people in religion, for, as yet at least, he has not ventured to declare himself in favour of dis-establishing and dis-endowing the Church of England, though he has not scrupled to throw out vague hints that he may do so hereafter, as a lure to enlist new recruits to take the place of old followers he has driven from his standard. It may therefore be fairly assumed that, at present at all events, Mr. Gladstone sees nothing wrong or unjust in the existence of a State provision for teaching religion, if it is made in such a manner as to inflict no hardship on any part of the people, and I even venture to hope that on this point his opinions may not differ widely from my own.

To me it has always appeared very difficult to understand how some of those who insist upon the necessity of making ample provision for the secular education of the whole people, can hold it to be wrong that any provision whatever should be made for their being instructed in religion. I am far from being indifferent to the great benefits arising from the general diffusion in a nation of that secular knowledge, and that cultivation of the understanding by which men are rendered more able to engage with success in all the various employments of life, and to serve better both themselves and the community. But experience has only too clearly proved that mere intellectual instruction is not sufficient either to make men good subjects to the State, or to secure their own welfare. For both these objects they require to be taught the great truths of religion, and their duty to God, a sense of which can alone subdue the "unruly wills and affections" of mankind; indeed, for the peace, order, and prosperity of a community, it is far more important that its members should generally understand and feel their responsibility to their Creator, than that they should be well instructed in secular knowledge. As, therefore, it is found that, without the intervention of the state, secular instruction cannot be made as general as it ought to be, so also, with regard to religious instruction, it seems to me very clear that it is of great advantage to a nation that some means of supplying it should be provided beyond those which can be furnished by the unaided exertions of individuals. In both cases individual exertion ought to be encouraged, and as much freedom as possible should be given to those who may not be satisfied with the instruction provided by authority, but in both also voluntary efforts require to be aided, and this is especially true with regard to religious instruction, since those who stand in most need of it, are just those who do not feel their want, and will not therefore contribute to the cost of supplying it. We know also that the principal dissenting Churches find it necessary, for carrying on their work with success, to secure for themselves, by private benevolence or otherwise, at least some property yielding an income not dependent on the annual contributions

of their adherents to assist in meeting their
expenses.

Unless the views I have now stated are altogether false, Mr. Gladstone made a great mistake in declaring that the property held by the Established Church of Ireland must cease to be employed for the purpose for which it was intended, of providing for the religious instruction of the people. It had failed to accomplish its purpose because it was held exclusively by a Church of which the services were refused by a large majority of the nation, but this fault would have been corrected, as I have shown, if the revenue, which had long been devoted to the support of the Protestant Establishment, had been applied to the religious instruction of the people by means of the three Churches, to one or other of which they almost all belong. The principle of making public provision for the teaching of religion would thus have been maintained in Ireland, as it is in England and in Scotland, and certainly the people of Ireland have not less need of aid in meeting the cost of supporting their clergy than those of the two other parts of the United Kingdom. To make a great change in the law relating to the Irish Church on the plea that this was required by justice to the Irish people, and, at the same time, to insist that they should be denied an advantage which is enjoyed by their fellow subjects on the other side of St. George's Channel, was to be guilty of a most flagrant inconsistency. Nor could it be pleaded in excuse for this inconsistency that the property was wanted for some other great national object; on the contrary, when the Disestablishment Act was passed, what to do with the money it made disposable became a serious embarrassment to its authors, and, as no scheme for turning it to account could be agreed upon, the decision as to how it should be applied was postponed. Since that time, a considerable proportion of the large sum expected to be available for objects of public advantage, it is to be feared, has been improvidently wasted, little, if any, real permanent good having been effected by means of it. In denouncing the policy of settling the question on the principle timidly hinted at by Lord Mayo when he spoke of "levelling up," Mr. Gladstone did not even attempt to show that this policy would be either ill-calculated to promote the true welfare of the Irish people, or opposed to their wishes. What he said against it was really little more than an assertion, unsupported by argument, that nothing ought to be done in this matter contrary to the opinions of those who condemn all applications of public money to religious purposes.

No one but Mr. Gladstone himself can know what was his motive for acting in the manner I have described on the question of the Irish Church in 1868; it cannot, therefore, be asserted that his object in what he did was to overthrow the existing administration, and bring his own party into power, but whether this was, or was not, his object, it certainly was the effect of the course he adopted; and, if it was the end it was designed to accomplish, it could not have been more skilfully contrived for that purpose. By insisting on the immediate and absolute disestablishment of the Irish Church, and that the whole of its property, except what was necessary to meet existing claims, should be applied to purposes unconnected with the teaching of religion, the Opposition both forced the ministers to resist their demand, and secured for themselves powerful allies in the contest they thus made inevitable. They were sure to gain the eager support of the advocates of what is called "the voluntary principle," who regard all religious endowments, whether in England, in Scotland, or in Ireland, as abuses to be swept away as soon as possible, and of those who with an intolerance, equal to that for which they denounce the Church of Rome, insist that because (as they assert) the teaching of the Roman Catholic Church is false, the State cannot, without sin, allow those who profess it to enjoy the same advantages with regard to religious instruction, and to the education of their children, as Christians of other denominations. With these allies Mr. Gladstone and his followers defeated the ministry of Mr. Disraeli, first in the House of Commons, and afterwards more completely on the hustings, where the battle of parties turned mainly on the question of the Irish Church. The defeat of the Disraeli ministry in the general election forced it to make way for another under Mr. Gladstone, and among the first measures of the latter, when the new Parliament met, was one for the disestablishment of the Irish Church. The Bill which was brought forward in the House of Commons by Mr. Gladstone in 1869, was strictly in accordance with the principle he had contended for in 1868, and provided that neither from the property which had been held by the Church which was to be disestablished, nor from public money derived from any other sources, should any state aid in the future be granted either to Protestants or to Roman Catholics for the support of their clergy, or for religious instruction, except so far as was necessary to guard against the injustice of depriving of what they enjoyed those who were entitled to advantages under the existing arrangements. Public opinion being so strongly, and, as I think, so properly, decided against maintaining the Protestant Church Establishment of Ireland in the position it then held, while the Conservative party had lost the opportunity of proposing any better scheme for putting an end to what was felt to be indefensible in the existing state of things, this Bill was passed through both Houses of Parliament, with little difficulty.

The Disestablishment Act of 1869, which was thus passed, had been recommended to the House of Commons with an exceedingly eloquent description of the great good it was to accomplish, and with a jubilant prediction that it would be accepted by the Irish people as a generous concession, and would win back their hearts to the Imperial Government. Unhappily this prediction proved to be altogether delusive. Instead of exciting any sense of gratitude to the Imperial Government and Parliament, the passing of what we had been confidently assured would prove a healing measure, was followed almost immediately by a more general display on the part of the Irish people, than had previously been witnessed, of feelings of disaffection to the Crown and of hostility to the British nation. The rapidity with which an increase of agitation and of crimes in Ireland followed Mr. Gladstone's accession to power, and the change of policy he prided himself on having introduced, was most remarkable. I have already quoted what he said in March 1868 as to the improvement which had then taken place in the condition of Ireland, and especially as to the sentiment of attachment to law and order which had grown up in the last generation. Compare this account of the state of Ireland in March 1868 with that which he has lately given of its condition, just two years afterwards in 1870. In his speech on the third reading of the Crimes Bill on the 7th of

July 1887, he justified himself for opposing that Bill, though he had himself carried one of a similar, or rather much stronger, description in 1870, on the ground that the state of Ireland in respect of the prevalence of crimes in 1870 was much worse than it has been during the present year. He said, "The point in 1870, as I have said, was not simply the height to which agrarian crime had reached, but the rate at which it was increasing . . . . . In 1866 the number of reported agrarian offences was 87. That was increased rapidly in 1867, 1868, and 1869. In 1869 the number was 767, or nearly ninefold what it had been in 1866, and even in 1869 the movement was most remarkable, because, while in the first quarter of 1869, from January to March, there were 101 reported agrarian offences; in the last quarter from October to December, which may fairly be compared with the same quarter, there were 540 such offences. Thus the increase of agrarian crime was more than fivefold within the course of a single year." In this statement Mr. Gladstone has greatly exaggerated the increase of agrarian crimes in the time he was speaking of, because, with his usual carelessness about accuracy, he has taken figures from the returns as to these crimes presented to Parliament, which seemed to serve his immediate purpose, without taking the trouble to advert to a memorandum which Mr. Balfour laid before the House of Commons on the 9th of May, and which explains that, in consequence of changes that have been made in the mode of preparing these returns, they are useless for the purpose of comparing the number of crimes committed in the years referred to by Mr. Gladstone, without large corrections, which there do not appear to be the means of supplying.

But though there is characteristic exaggeration in Mr. Gladstone's statement, there can be no doubt that in 1870 there had been within a short time a lamentable increase in the number of agrarian crimes committed in Ireland, and that, early in that year, a spirit of lawlessness had arisen, which called for the stern measure of repression passed by Parliament at the instance of Mr. Gladstone's government. This was a sad change for the worse from the state of things in Ireland only two years before, when Mr. Gladstone was able to speak with just hopefulness of the good effects to be looked for from " the sentiment of attachment to law and order" which had grown up among its people in the last generation. There is no reason to be surprised that within a year of the time when Mr. Gladstone had won the blind confidence and enthusiastic applause of the House of Commons by his glowing description of the blessings of peace, contentment, and prosperity, his policy was to confer upon Ireland, his first and most important measure should have thus signally failed to do the good he expected; the character of the measure, and the manner in which it was carried, sufficiently account for the failure. Of the character of the measure, and the want of political wisdom it displayed, I have already spoken; but, great as were its faults, they have probably contributed less than the manner in which it was carried to cause the evils it has been followed by.

The defeat of Mr. Disraeli's government on the resolutions moved by Mr. Gladstone led to the Irish Church becoming the subject on which the conflict of parties mainly turned in the ensuing general election. This must have done much harm in Ireland, where the religious animosities of its people have so long been a fruitful source of evil, even if the contest had been carried on without any unusual bitterness, but it was not so. In the multitude of meetings held during the elections, many of the Opposition candidates spoke with unmeasured violence against the Established Church of Ireland, against the ministers who had given it their support when assailed in the House of Commons, against the Orange party, and even against the Irish Protestants generally, whom they seemed to confound with it. In the Lancashire meetings especially, Mr. Gladstone exhausted his great powers of eloquence in describing the evils that had been brought upon Ireland by the power of England, and the wrongs which, as he asserted, the Irish people had long suffered, and were still suffering, from the system of government it had compelled them to endure. This system of government he likened to a upas tree having three branches that must be cut down, the Church being only the first which had to be dealt with. Such language was only too well calculated to stir up feelings of hatred to the Imperial Government and the British nation, in the minds of the excitable Irish people, and to lead them to regard the overthrow of the

Church establishment, not as a concession they ought to be grateful for, but as a tardy surrender of what had long been unjustly withheld from them. And this surrender they might naturally conclude to have been due, not to the feeling towards them in England having become more kindly than it had been, nor to an increased sense of justice, but to intimidation, when they were told that the concession made to them had been brought " within the range of practical politics" by the murder of a policeman at Manchester, and by the atrocious outrage at Clerkenwell. From the passing of such a measure as that for the disestablishment of the Irish Church, recommended and carried by such speeches as those made by Mr. Gladstone in Lancashire and in the House of Commons, no result could reasonably be looked for but that which actually followed from it; disaffection became more bitter, and was felt by a greater number of the population of Ireland; and there was an increase of lawlessness and of outrages which compelled the ministers of the Crown to ask Parliament for new powers for their suppression, when it again assembled after the passing of their " healing measure." Such was the failure of the first step taken by Mr. Gladstone after he had persuaded Parliament to entrust him with unlimited power to carry into effect his Irish policy. Unfortunately, it was only the prelude to the still more disastrous failure of his subsequent measures. In the next chapter, I will consider the character, and the effect, of the legislation he introduced as to the tenure of land.

CHAPTER IV.

IRISH LAND ACTS OF 1870 AND 1881.

In the last chapter I have endeavoured to show that in the years 1868 and 1869 Mr. Gladstone threw away a great opportunity of conferring benefit upon Ireland by his conduct on the question of the Irish Church, and that the Act for its dis-establishment, passed by his advice, accomplished a much-needed reform in such a manner as to deprive it of the greater part of the advantages it ought to have produced. I have now to consider the legislation with regard to the occupation of land in Ireland, which he prevailed on Parliament to sanction, with the consequences which have followed from its adoption.

There can be no doubt that in 1870, when Mr. Gladstone and his colleagues proceeded, by introducing their Land Bill, to deal with what he had described as the second branch of the upas tree that over-shadowed Ireland, the law as to the relations of the owners and occupiers of land in that part of the United Kingdom stood much in need of amendment. But as the subject was one of acknowledged difficulty, great care ought to have been taken to consider what were the real faults of the law as it then stood, and how they could be best corrected. The Act at that time in force was one which had been carried in 1860, by an administration of which Mr. Gladstone and several of those who were his colleagues in 1870 had been members. It entirely altered the whole system of the former laws of Ireland as to the tenure of land, and expressly declared that for the future the relations between the owners and occupiers of land were to rest solely upon contract. This Act had not worked well, and in 1867 a Bill for its amendment (or rather for its repeal, and the substitution of different provisions in its place), which had been drawn up by Mr. Tighe Hamilton, was brought into the House of Lords by the late Lord Clanricarde, and on his motion was referred to a Select Committee, which inquired into the working of the law as it then stood, and into the plan suggested for its improvement. Some very valuable information on these points was obtained by the Committee, and they afterwards proceeded, in that and the following Session, to consider the Bill referred to them in connection with the evidence they had collected. The conclusion they came to was that the unsatisfactory working of Lord Cardwell's Irish Land Act of 1860 was not due to its being wrong in principle, but to many serious faults in its provisions for carrying this principle into effect. The mode of correcting these faults proposed by Mr. T. Hamilton was approved by the Committee, and having made a good many amendments in his Bill which had been referred to them, they unanimously recommended that it should be adopted by the House.

The following were the chief defects in Lord Cardwell's Act which were found to have interfered with its successful operation. It had left the law obscure on some important points, and much inconvenience had arisen from doubts as to what was its real effect; in adopting the sound principle of recognising contract between the parties as the basis of the relations between landlords and tenants, it failed to provide any means for clearly and easily ascertaining what were

the terms of contracts that had been entered into;
it discouraged written contracts by leaving them
subject to needless expense, and by allowing the
same force to verbal, and even to implied, contracts
as to written ones; it further practically discouraged
the grant of leases for terms of years, by not providing for either party any easy and effectual mode
of enforcing the performance of the agreements
they had entered into; and lastly, while the above
defects tended to create disputes between landlords
and tenants, no sufficient provision was made for
having these disputes promptly and cheaply decided.
Such were the chief faults of Lord Cardwell's Act
of 1860, which till 1870 governed the relations of
landlords and tenants in Ireland. The most serious
grievance arising from them to which tenants were
exposed was that the state of the law made it
difficult for them to improve their land without
the risk of losing the money and labour expended
upon it, either by being turned out of their holdings,
or by having an increased rent demanded for them
on account of the increased value their exertions
had conferred on them. The law, it is true, allowed
agreements to be made which would have relieved
tenants from this grievance, but owing to their

needless cost, and the want of any proper arrangement for recording them, written agreements for this purpose were in fact seldom made. Hence great injustice was occasionally done to tenants who had improved their land, though the cases in which this happened were certainly exceptions to the general rule; and sometimes even, when there might be an appearance of injustice being done by the demand of increased rent in consequence of improvements made by the tenants, none was really committed, because the demand was in accordance with a previous understanding between the parties. Tenants not unfrequently made improvements with an express understanding that, after they had enjoyed the full benefit of them for a certain time, the landlord was to have his share of the increased value given to his land.

The principle of such an agreement is quite fair and reasonable. It is that of the leases which used generally to be given in Scotland and the North of England, before the passing of the Agricultural Holdings Act made it unsafe for landowners to continue to make an arrangement with their tenants, which during a long course of years had been found equally beneficial to both parties. By these leases the owners of land gave up the power of resuming possession of it, generally for nineteen years in Scotland, and for twenty-one years in England, and, in consideration of doing so, they expected to receive it back at the end of the term agreed upon in improved condition. The farmers, on the other hand, with the security thus given to them, were enabled to effect very important improvements on taking their farms, of which they recovered the cost by increased produce before their leases expired. Sometimes it was agreed that the landlord should bear part of the expense of important and costly improvements, either by an allowance to the tenant at the time they were made, or by a money payment on the expiration of the lease. Mainly through the operation of this system, a large part of Scotland, which a century and a half ago yielded only low rents to the owners, and a hard living to the occupiers, under very rude cultivation, has been gradually improved till its rental rose to probably four or five times what it was. These rents were paid by a tenantry, who though now suffering severely from bad times, have long been among the most skilful and prosperous agriculturists in the world, in whose employment the labouring population enjoyed a very high degree of comfort, and have been remarkable for their intelligence, industry, and orderly character. In the North of England the same mode of letting land has proved equally successful, and the well known and able agriculturist, the late Mr. Grey, of Dilston, in an article on the state of agriculture in Northumberland which he contributed to the Journal of the Royal Agricultural Society in 1840, after describing the advantages all the parties concerned derived from this system, concludes his observations upon it by expressing his belief "that to the custom of letting land on long leases, more than to any other cause, though of course in conjunction with other causes, this county is indebted for its rapid improvement and high state of cultivation." *

But in Scotland and the North of England these good results have been achieved by means of leases of which the conditions were freely settled by the parties concerned, and clearly stated in writing, so that there could be no dispute as to how long the tenant was to have the full enjoyment of the improvements he might make, and when the land was again to revert to

* Journal of the Royal Society of England, vol. ii, p. 157.

the unrestricted possession of the owner, or if he was then to pay a part of the cost of improvements which had been effected, what that payment was to be. Unfortunately in Ireland it has been otherwise. These improvements have usually been effected by tenants only on an understanding of the vaguest kind, that they should be allowed to hold their land, without being called upon to pay higher rents, long enough to repay themselves. Even when a more precise agreement had been made as to how long a tenant was to be allowed to hold land he had reclaimed or improved without an advance of rent being demanded, the agreement was almost always merely verbal, so that its terms were apt to be forgotten before the time came when it gave the landlord a right to ask for a higher rent. Very often by that time those who had made the agreement were dead, and it was natural that those who had succeeded them as landlord and tenant should sometimes differ as to what had been agreed upon by those who went before them. In some of the cases in which the fiercest disputes have taken place between landlords and tenants as to the right of the former to raise their rents, there is every reason to think

that both parties honestly believed themselves to
have justice on their side. But it was often otherwise; there were too many cases in which landlords availed themselves of their legal right, in
order unjustly to deprive tenants holding land
only from year to year of the fruits of their labour,
as, on the other hand, there were also many in
which the tenants resorted to violence in resisting
claims they knew to be just. The existence of
written and clear agreements would have averted
these disputes.

The evidence brought before Lord Clanricarde's
Committee clearly showed that the faults in the
law I have described were the main cause of
almost all the difficulties and disputes that had
arisen between Irish landlords and tenants. And
it was much to the credit of both classes that
these difficulties and disputes had not been
greater and more frequent. For it was the
general opinion of the witnesses who were examined that, notwithstanding the defects in the
then existing law which they complained of, the
relations between landlords and tenants in Ireland
were, on the whole, far more satisfactory than was
commonly supposed. It was not denied that evils

existed, that neither landlords nor tenants always performed their duties as they ought. On the one side there was sometimes a harsh and even unjust exercise of legal rights; on the other a disposition to evade the due performance of their agreements; but it was stated that such cases were only exceptions, and that, as a rule, Irish landlords and tenants lived together upon terms of mutual good will. It was also shown that, while the improvement of land was not going on so fast as might have been wished, and there were many landlords who were unable or unwilling to execute works that ought to have been done by them rather than by their tenants, still a steady and decided progress had been going on during the time that Lord Cardwell's Land Act was in force; in those ten years a notable advance had been accomplished in Irish agriculture, and large sums of money had been expended by landlords in improving their estates.

The Bill, which Lord Clanricarde's Committee recommended the House of Lords to adopt, would have corrected the faults of the Act of 1860, without departing from the principle on which it was founded. It had for its main object to give to the owners and occupiers of land freedom to settle with each other as they might think fit the conditions on which it was to be held, but requiring that all agreements of that kind should be made in writing, and should be recorded in such a manner as to make them always easy to be referred to. Arrangements were made by its provisions for enabling the parties concerned to enter into these agreements with exceedingly little trouble or expense. The Bill would also have encouraged the grant of leases for terms of years, by greatly reducing their cost, and by providing for cheaper and more effectual methods of enforcing the covenants they contained than then existed. It would not have conferred upon the tenant the right of claiming compensation for anything he might choose to call an improvement, because it was clearly shown that by giving such a right much injustice would have been done to the owners of land, who in consequence might be required after a lapse of years to pay for works executed without their knowledge, and which might have diminished instead of increasing the value of their property. This is by no means uncommonly the effect in Ireland of what are called improvements, as, for instance, when the tenant of a holding which is already too small allows a part of it to be occupied by a son or a son-in-law for whom he builds an additional cabin. The injustice there would be in compelling a landlord to pay for the erection of a building of this sort, by which his property would be positively deteriorated, is obvious; the cases are not less numerous in which the claims for improvements set up by Irish tenants, and resisted by their landlords, have been of this unreasonable character than those in which reasonable claims have been unfairly rejected. These considerations induced the Committee to refuse to insert in the Bill they reported to the House of Lords any provisions to confer on tenants an absolute right to compensation for all so-called improvements, but it contained clauses which would have given new and important facilities for effecting real improvements, by agreement between the owners and the occupiers of land. Landlords would have been enabled to borrow money for improvements when their tenants were willing to pay an increased rent to meet the charge for interest on the loans so raised; or if the parties preferred it, the execution of improvements agreed upon might have been left to the tenants, a charge for their cost being made on the land in their favour. The arrangements by which such agreements were to have been entered into, and registered to guard against subsequent disputes, would have been exceedingly simple and so little costly, that it might safely have been left to the common interest of the parties concerned to ensure their being taken advantage of.

The Bill I have described was so well drawn by Mr. Tighe Hamilton, and so much pains had been taken by the Committee to improve its details, that if it had been passed I am convinced it would have done all that legislation could do for putting the letting of land in Ireland on a good footing for the future. But it would not have affected existing tenancies, and these would, in my opinion, have required to be dealt with by a separate measure. I have already recognised the fact that under the former law gross injustice was sometimes inflicted on Irish tenants by depriving them without compensation of the fruits of the labour and money they had expended in improving their land, and, though the cases in which such injustice was done were far less common than was generally supposed, they occurred quite often enough to call urgently for a remedy. A complete one might have been afforded without any violation of the rights of property, by enacting that where the owners of land had so acted as to create in their tenants a reasonable expectation of being allowed the advantage of improvements, this should be recognised as constituting a legal and binding agreement to that effect. For example, when it could be shown that within a certain period improvements had been made by the tenant, which it might fairly be concluded he would not have undertaken without the expectation of enjoying their benefit, and that no warning against his doing so had been given by the owner of the land, or by his agent, it would have been perfectly consistent with the principles acted upon by our courts of equity, as well as with natural justice, to recognise the claim of the tenant to compensation, either in money, or by being allowed to retain his land without an increase of rent long enough to recover his outlay. The mere knowledge that such protection could and would be granted by the courts of law when it was needed, would usually have prevented injustice from being attempted; probably, therefore, there would have been but few applications for the interference of the courts, and in no great number of years, under the amended law, they must have ceased altogether.

In the preceding paragraphs, I have endeavoured to explain what were the faults of the law of Ireland with regard to the occupation of land as it stood when Mr. Gladstone undertook to improve it, and how those faults might have been corrected, and the real grievances of the tenants might have been redressed, without disturbing the existing relations between the owners and the occupiers of land, and without the slightest infringement on the rights of property. This explanation has extended to a greater length than I could have wished, but this I have been unable to avoid, because the mischievous character of the Land Acts of 1870 and of 1881, which I desire to expose, cannot be properly appreciated without clearly understanding in what manner a settlement of the Irish land question upon sound principles might have been attempted with good prospects of success, when this vicious legislation was begun. The Land Acts of 1870 and 1881 are founded on principles of legislation and on views of policy the very opposite of those to which effect would have been given by passing the Bill recommended by the Lords' Committee in 1868, together with such a supplementary measure as would have been required to complete it. Instead of attempting, like the Bill of the Lords' Committee, to correct the faults which had been found to interfere with the successful working of Lord Cardwell's Act of 1860, the Land Act of 1870 contained no single provision directed to that object. It did not expressly repeal the former Act, but it contained provisions of a novel character, which rendered practically inoperative (at least with regard to small holdings) its main principle, that contract was to be free and the basis of the relations between landlords and tenants. Instead of being allowed freely to settle with each other on what conditions land was to be held, rules were laid down from which the parties concerned were to have no power to depart in making agreements as to the occupation of small portions of land. Again, instead of seeking, like the Bill recommended by the Lords' Committee, to remove occasions for dispute between the owners and the occupiers of land, and to lead them to see that they have a common interest in its improvement, the Act of 1870 shows throughout that it must have been drawn up on the assumption that landlords and tenants are natural enemies, and that the main object of the new law ought to be to protect the latter from the injustice with which they were sure to be generally treated.

The provisions of an Act framed in this spirit were but too sure to create that hostility between the two classes which it assumed to be general, but which, as I have shown, was in reality only found to exist in exceptional cases under the former law. There was another and a far more important difference than any I have yet mentioned between the Land Act of 1870 and the legislation on this subject which had been previously proposed. The latter, in every amendment it would have made in the law, would have carefully respected the rights of property; the Act of 1870, on the contrary, deprived the owners of land, without any compensation, of a considerable part of its value. While the measure was under discussion, it was denied that it would have any such effect, but since it has been in operation the fact that it has very considerably diminished the value of land to its owners has become too clear to be disputed. This diminution of the value of land to those whose rights as owners had never before been questioned, was produced in two ways by the Act of 1870. It arose partly from the retrospective character of the clauses, which conferred on tenants generally a right they had not previously enjoyed of claiming compensation for improvements effected on their land, and yet failed to provide any sufficient precautions against unjust claims being preferred. Much injustice was inflicted on the owners of land by these clauses, and the most improving owners were the greatest sufferers; but still greater wrong was done to them by the provisions which gave to the tenant a claim to compensation for "disturbance," if the owner chose to resume possession of his land when the time for which it had been let had expired. By these provisions, landlords were not only mulcted of part of their property,* but they were practi-

---

* To show that Mr. Gladstone has distinctly admitted the fact that his Land Act of 1870 took away from the owners of land in Ireland a part of their property, and made it over to their tenants, I would refer to the following passages of the speech he made on the 7th of April 1881 in bringing in his Land Bill of that year. He said, " With a supply of land in the market so much less than

cally deprived of the only effectual mode of enforcing their right to what was left to them, and of preventing their land from being injured by the barbarous and wasteful practices to which Irish

the demand, you have a state of things in which it is well worth the while of a man who has not got land as a means of getting a regular subsistence and livelihood to pay for obtaining it. That willingness of the incoming tenant to pay enters distinctly into the interest of the outgoing tenant." . . . . (Hansard, Vol. cxlx., p. 900.) And a little further on in the same speech he says, " Before the Land Act of 1870 the tenancy was determinable upon a certain notice at the close of each year at the sole will of the landlord. . . . . What the tenant had to assign was so small that the assignment was little worth giving or receiving. But in the Land Act . . . . . to defend the tenant in possession of his holding, and to render it difficult for the landlord capriciously to get rid of him, we proceeded to enact a scale of compensation for disturbance, without which the tenant could not be reassured. That being so, a valuable consideration was, by the Act of 1870, evidently tacked on to every yearly tenancy in Ireland . . . . . tenant right has become something sensible and considerable. The actual sale of tenant right . . . . has grown and spread in Ireland." (Page 908.) This statement is quite clear and quite correct, and of course the " valuable consideration which was by the Act of 1870 evidently tacked on to every yearly tenancy in Ireland," was substracted from what previously belonged to the landlord. The total value of the property was not increased, therefore whatever was added to the interest in it of the tenant was so much deducted from that of the landlord. And this deduction, as Mr. Gladstone said, " has become something sensible and considerable." Accounts frequently appear in the newspapers of large sums being paid for the interest of tenants in their holdings; sometimes, if I am not misinformed, more is paid cultivators are so prone to resort. And it was also by these provisions of the Act of 1870 that a beginning was made in the introduction of what has been called "the dual ownership" of land, a system which is now almost universally admitted to be so injurious, that, in order to get rid of it, Parliament (as we are informed) is to be asked to sanction measures which are not less opposed to sound policy, and which I am persuaded will prove, if they are adopted, not less mischievous than the enactments by which it was established.

Having thus shown how wide a difference of principle there is between the Bill recommended to the House of Lords by its Committee in 1868, and the Irish Land Act of 1870, I will now endeavour to prove that the policy of the last was so obviously unsound that it ought never to have received the sanction of Parliament, and that it has been the chief cause of all the worst evils which have afflicted Ireland ever since it was

---

for it than the landowner could get for what is left for him, that is to say, more than half his property has been confiscated. It is singular that only nine years after Mr. Gladstone had assured the Irish landowners that they were not to be injured by his measure of 1870, he should himself have explained to Parliament how it had deprived them of a large part of their property.

passed. But before I enter into this argument I must make the preliminary remark, that it is hard to understand why it was that when Mr. Gladstone proposed to Parliament an entire change in the laws of Ireland relating to the occupation of land, he took no notice whatever of the labours of Lord Clanricarde's Committee. That Committee included among its members Irish Peers who had great practical knowledge of the rural affairs of their own country, and also peers who, having no personal connexion with Ireland, were free from any bias of private interest, and therefore likely to form an impartial judgment from the full information before them as to how this difficult subject might best be dealt with in order to do justice to tenants and landlords, and to promote the real welfare of both. This Committee, after taking great pains during two sessions (as I have already mentioned) to collect the best information they could obtain, and to consider the clauses of the Bill referred to them, unanimously recommended that it should be passed with the amendments they had made in it. If Mr. Gladstone, when he brought forward his own measure was aware of the inquiry that had taken place, and of the conclusions come to by the Committee, it would have been fitting that he should have taken some notice of them, even if it had been only by stating his reasons for rejecting them. If he was ignorant of these proceedings, this would show that he brought forward a measure of extreme importance, which must necessarily have a powerful effect for good or for evil on the future condition of Ireland, without having studied the subject with the care it was his duty to bestow upon it.

Reverting to the question as to whether the policy of the Land Act of 1870 was right, I have to observe that in his various speeches Mr. Gladstone has defended the measure mainly on the ground that it was rendered necessary by the existence of an excessive competition for land, and of what he called " a hunger for land" among the Irish people. I agree with Mr. Gladstone in believing that there was in a considerable part of Ireland an excessive competition for land, and that an intense desire to possess it, which might well be described as " a hunger," prevailed among the population. Nor do I doubt that this state of things was attended with deplorable results, but I contend that the Land Act of 1870 was calculated not to abate, but to aggravate the evils that were justly complained of. On the subject of this "land hunger," Mr. Gladstone in bringing in his second Land Bill on the 7th of April 1881, said,* " that old and standing evil of Ireland, that land hunger, which must not be described as if it were merely an infirmity of the people, and really means land scarcity, still continues to import into the agricultural relations of Ireland difficulties with which as yet we have not been able completely to deal." This is perfectly true; "land scarcity" was the real difficulty to be contended with, the available land in Ireland was not sufficient, under the system of cultivation which generally prevailed there, and in the deficiency of other kinds of employment, to maintain the existing population in reasonable comfort. The fact was correctly stated by Mr. Gladstone, but he does not appear to have perceived what was the conclusion to be drawn from it as to how the condition of the people could be improved, though this seems to be very clear. The Government and Parliament had no power either to increase

* Hansard, vol. colx., p. 898.

the extent of land in Ireland, or to diminish the evils arising from an excessive competition for it so long as its "scarcity"—that is to say, its insufficiency to meet the wants of its inhabitants—continues. Their condition, therefore, could only be improved in one of two ways: first, by the better cultivation of the soil, so as to obtain from it a larger produce to maintain the population; or, secondly, by leading a part of that population to seek for a better livelihood either by emigration, or by directing more of their labour at home to other occupations instead of to agriculture. There was plenty of room for improvement in both these ways. I have already referred to the bad cultivation of the soil which has been described as being in general so unskilful and ineffective that some competent judges have asserted that if the cultivation of Irish farms was as good as that of average English farms their produce would be doubled. This may be, and probably is, an exaggeration, but it is certain that the ordinary mode of cultivating the soil in Ireland is so inferior to that which is to be found in most parts of Europe that it may almost be called barbarous. An improvement in agriculture was therefore greatly needed, and would have done much for the welfare of the population. Much might also have been done for it by leading the Irish people to look less exclusively to tilling the soil for their livelihood, and more to earning it by other kinds of labour. It is certain that there was, and still is, an ample field for the profitable employment of a large number of the people of Ireland in other directions instead of in agriculture, if they had enough enterprise and energy to take advantage of it.

Sir R. Kane showed long ago, in his excellent book, that their own country is rich in natural resources which would well repay the intelligent application of industry to their development. When, therefore, Mr. Gladstone, in 1870, undertook to deal with the laws of Ireland relating to the tenure of land, the two principal objects his legislation ought to have aimed at were to promote a change for the better in the generally wretched cultivation of the soil, and to lead the population to trust less to the occupation of land, and look more to other modes of earning a subsistence than they had hitherto done. Instead of being calculated to answer these purposes, the

Act for which he obtained the sanction of Parliament tended inevitably to produce the very opposite effect. Its purpose was artificially to keep down rents, but, in seeking to do this, the framers of the law in question were attempting to accomplish what was impossible, and what, if it had been possible, would have done harm instead of good. Nothing can be more clearly proved by experience than that just as laws have been found powerless to keep down the price of commodities to an arbitrary maximum, even when enforced by the guillotine, as in the first French revolution, so also they always fail long to keep down the real cost of land to those who hold it below what its price would be if it were left to be determined in the natural way by the demand for it, as compared with the available supply. If rents for land are settled by the authority of law at rates below its real market value, occupiers, either by selling their right of occupation, or by borrowing money on its security, seldom fail very soon to burthen it with fresh charges in addition to the legal rent, which raise its cost to the actual holders to that which is determined by competition. And, if rents could be effectively kept down by law, this would prove injurious instead of advantageous to the community, and even to that class for whose benefit such an artificial system was attempted. An advance of rents is the natural consequence of the advance of a nation in civilization and prosperity, and it is not only a consequence of such progress, but one of its most efficient causes. As land becomes dearer the occupiers are compelled to make greater exertions in order to obtain from the soil the means of paying for the land they hold, as well as win their own subsistence, while some are driven to seek for their livelihood by other occupations; thus improved cultivation is gradually introduced, as well as the division of labour, and in both ways the progress of the community is advanced.

Necessity, it has been well said, is the mother of invention; it is no less true that the pressure of necessity, and of a desire to better their condition, has afforded the stimulus by which men have been gradually raised from barbarism to the highest state of civilization to which they have as yet anywhere attained, and which, we trust, is still leading them on to something higher. This is the natural condition of human society, as ordered by divine wisdom, and when a government steps in and attempts by artificial aid directly to increase the welfare of any class of its subjects, and to relieve them from difficulties they have to contend with, instead of being content with endeavouring to remove any obstacles which stand in the way of their raising themselves by their own exertions to a better position, the ultimate result is invariably to do harm instead of good to those to whom such injudicious assistance is granted.

These considerations lead me to the conclusion that the Land Act of 1870 was based on a principle essentially unsound, and its practical operation has been rendered more injurious than it might otherwise have been by the peculiar circumstances of Ireland. The improvement of agriculture was one of its most pressing wants, and this improvement was beginning to take place, but, in direct contradiction to what is generally asserted and believed, in almost every case in which important improvements had been effected, they were due to the exertions of enlightened and energetic landlords or agents, and not to the voluntary action of the tenants. As a general rule, though, of course, there were exceptions to it, these improvements had been accomplished by overcoming the resistance (most commonly passive, but not unfrequently active) of ignorant tenants to any change in practices to which they were accustomed. These practices were no longer so barbarous as those of the Irish cultivators in the days of Queen Elizabeth, described by the poet Spenser, but were still wasteful and improvident, and in many parts of Ireland the small farmers were so wedded to the unskilful mode of cultivating the soil to which they had been accustomed, that to induce them to depart from it, and to introduce a better system, was a matter of extreme difficulty. The late Mr. Bence Jones, in his "Life's Work in Ireland," has given a most interesting account of the difficulties he had thus to encounter in introducing agricultural improvements on his estate in the county of Cork, of the patient and persevering efforts by which this work was accomplished, and of its complete success, as well in adding to his own income, as in still more remarkably increasing the welfare of his tenants, and of the labourers around him. By good, instead of by bad, management the productiveness of the land was so largely increased that both the owner and the occupier were better off than before. Mr. Mahoney has also published an account of a similar success achieved under the same difficulties as those Mr. Bence Jones had to contend with, and on many other estates, including some of the largest in Ireland, like improvements were going on. These improvements were due, partly to the expenditure of large sums of money by the owners of estates in draining, building, and other works, but still more to the use of their power and influence as landlords to restrain their tenants from resorting to some of the worst and most improvident of their traditional practices, and to require them to substitute better modes of cultivation. The good thus done was not confined to the properties on which it was directly the work of the owners; the estates of judicious and improving landlords, became centres from which improvement was gradually spreading in many parts of Ireland, as the example of the better managed farms was beginning to make some impression on the surrounding occupiers, difficult as they were to move. This is an important and significant fact, and it is another which is still more so, that few, if any, examples could be found of improved cultivation in Ireland which have not been due directly or indirectly to the efforts of intelligent and educated owners or managers of considerable estates.

In what I have just said I have been referring chiefly to those parts of Ireland in which the soil and climate are not unfavourable to arable cultivation. But there are, as it is well known, some districts of a different character, in which from their ungenial climate, and their large proportion of sterile soil, such cultivation never can be carried on with advantage. In these districts the state of things was far less promising than in those to which nature has been kinder; but even in them some slight indications at least of improvement might be perceived in 1870, though the condition of the population was still, as it had been for a very long time, exceedingly wretched. Speaking of this population sixty-five years ago (for it is obvious the remark cannot have been intended to apply to the Irish people generally), Dr. Arnold said, ". . . I am puzzled beyond measure what to think about Ireland. What good can be done permanently with a people who literally do make man's life as cheap as beasts;

and who are content to multiply in idleness, and in such beggary that the failure of a crop brings them to starvation. I would venture to say that luxury never did half so much harm as the total indifference to comfort is doing in Ireland by leading to a propagation of the human race in a state of brutality."* Later accounts show that in the wet and stormy climate of the west and northwest of Ireland, the population, on lands generally mountainous and unproductive, has continued to live much in the same way as that deplored by Dr. Arnold, and the repeated attempts to relieve the constantly recurring distress in bad seasons, by private benevolence, or by aid from the State, has failed (as Mr. O'Connor Power said in the House of Commons in 1848) to do any permanent good. In 1870, as I have said, there were some faint symptoms of improvement ; in some cases those who were leading the wretched life Dr. Arnold has described were showing a new inclination to seek for relief from it by emigration, or migration to other parts of Ireland, and a few attempts were also being made to turn the land to better account. Both in these wilder districts, and in

* Dr. Arnold's Life, vol. i., p. 61, letter dated 21 October 1822.

those possessing greater natural advantages, but more especially in the latter, improvement in agriculture and in the condition of the population has been greatly checked by the novel and anomalous provision in the Land Act of 1870, whereby a right was conferred upon tenants to claim compensation for disturbance when required to give up their holdings at the close of the term for which they had been let by the owners. By this enactment the authority of landowners over their tenants was practically destroyed, and with it the only effectual means of carrying forward the work of improvement which had been begun, or even of preventing a retrograde movement. The security against being deprived of their holdings, which it was predicted would call forth a great increase of industry among Irish tenants, seems, on the contrary, according to the best accounts we have from eye-witnesses, to have led them to be less inclined than before to exchange their accustomed slovenly and wasteful mode of cultivation for a better one. And it has also very generally led them to use their right to their holdings as security to the banks for loans which now constitute a serious burthen on the farmers. And, while the new law has thus checked efforts to improve the land on the part of tenants, it has absolutely arrested them on the part of the owners; they could no longer be expected to spend their money in the improvement of their estates, and still less to borrow large sums for that purpose as they had been doing, when they were deprived of the powers necessary for the protection of their interest in their land.

The above remarks are applicable to the greater part of Ireland, but in the wilder districts to which I have referred, the evil worked by the Land Act seems to have been greater than elsewhere. The miserable condition in which the population of these districts has so long been accustomed to live, and which is described in the passage I have quoted from a letter of Dr. Arnold, is mainly owing to two causes; first, that in many of these districts the land is held in too small portions to yield a decent maintenance to the occupiers, under the disadvantages of soil and climate they have to contend with, even if they had no rent to pay; and secondly, that they are content to live in the wretched state they do without making any serious effort to raise themselves from it. The habitual misery of this part of the Irish population arising from these causes was sure to be, and in fact was, aggravated by the operation of the Land Act of 1870. It was intended to relieve their distress by securing them in the continued occupation of the land they held without being subject to an increase of rent. But this proved a cruel kindness to those who were its victims, for it practically encouraged them in their unfortunate disposition to cling to their small holdings of land, which, even with better cultivation than they knew how to bestow upon them, would have failed to maintain them in comfort, and which afforded them no means of profitable labour during great part of the year. It also encouraged them in the bad habit of looking for help, when the pressure of want came upon them, to others, and especially to the government, instead of to their own exertions. No mistake could be greater or more injurious to those it was intended to serve than to attempt, by such inadequate assistance as could be given, to enable a population in such a condition to persevere in struggling to maintain themselves in it, instead of seeking to obtain real welfare by a total change of their habits, and by their own strenuous exertions. Before the Land Act of 1870 was passed, we are told by so impartial and competent a witness as M. Molinari, that this desirable change was taking place ; very small holdings were being gradually consolidated, and other branches of industry were beginning to spring up, and to offer fresh openings for the profitable employment of labour. There is reason to fear that the passing of the above Act must have checked the progress of this most desirable change.

Still worse consequences than I have yet mentioned have followed from the passing of the Land Act of 1870; it has for a second time given dangerous encouragement to lawlessness, and it has done much to demoralise the Irish people. A great encouragement had already been given to lawlessness by the mode of carrying the Act for disestablishing the Church in 1869, a further and a greater encouragement was given to it by the Land Act of the following year. Both of these measures, and especially the last, were looked upon by the bulk of the Irish people as the fruits of successful agitation and intimidation; they had good reason for so regarding them, and there can be no doubt of the great encouragement which must thus have been given to the habits of lawlessness which have done so much harm to Ireland. The Land Act of 1870 was also the beginning of a new kind of demoralisation of the people (which has since been carried much further) by teaching them to look to stripping others of what rightfully belongs to them as the easiest way of improving their own condition. When this law took away from the owners, and gave to their tenants a considerable part of their landlord's property, it awoke in them (as it was sure to do) a desire for a larger share of it. When men have once been allowed—or, what is much worse, have been deliberately authorised by law—to take possession of what rightfully belongs to others, a taste for unjust acquisition is generally created, which can seldom be restrained so long as there remains anything that can be wrested from its owners to gratify the greed of spoilers. So it was in Ireland; I find no trace of any demand having been made by Irish tenants earlier than 1870 for the surrender to them by their landlords of any part of the property of which they were the lawful owners. So far as I am aware, till that time nothing more had been asked on behalf of the tenants than that they should be assured in some way or other of not being deprived of the fruits of whatever labour or money they might have expended in improving their farms. It is true that some of the changes in the law they demanded for this professed and legitimate object would, by their practical operation, have gone much further, but, in words at least, the full right of owners to their land had never been questioned. The new law had scarcely come into force before a change began to appear in the demeanour of tenants, and a cry that enough had not been given to them was raised in some quarters, though at first it was neither loud nor general. By degrees the demand for fresh concessions grew more importunate, and Mr. Gladstone's return to power in 1880 seemed to be the signal for its becoming violent and dangerous, probably, because the leading agitators, judging from their experience of the past, believed that by sufficient pressure anything might be wrung from him.

If this was their belief, it proved to be well founded, for though in 1870 Mr. Gladstone had solemnly assured the House of Commons that the Act then passed was to be a final settlement of the land question, and that "from the moment the measure is passed every Irishman, great and small, must be absolutely responsible for every contract into which he enters," in 1881 he brought in a new Bill, which made another large inroad on the property of the landlords, which virtually altered, greatly to their disadvantage, most of the contracts under which their land was held, and which it had been declared were to be held inviolable, and introduced the principle, which eleven years before he had denounced as altogether wrong and mischievous, of making the amount of rent to be paid for farms a matter to be decided by public authority, instead of by agreement between the parties concerned. This Bill was brought forward by Mr. Gladstone, and passed by Parliament in the session which followed an autumn and winter remarkable for the number of agrarian crimes committed in those months, for the violence of the language used by the agitators for Home Rule, and for the rise of the Land League into formidable power with the declaration of its leaders that the object they were striving for was the "Abolition of Landlordism." This phrase "the abolition of landlordism" is a singular one, and its real import seems not to have been sufficiently considered. It was probably devised to avoid using the ugly word of "confiscation," by substituting one which careless hearers might suppose to imply only that the abuse of the power of landlords was to be prevented. But this is an interpretation of the words which is quite inconsistent with the manner in which they have been used by Mr. Parnell and his followers; all their language, with the clear light thrown upon its meaning by what they have done, points to the fact that a general confiscation of Irish estates is the object they were steadily aiming at, nor has the purpose for which confiscation is desired been concealed. Mr. Parnell regards the landowners of Ireland as its "English garrison," which he wants to get rid of in order that British authority may be overthrown. He has told us he would not have "taken off his coat" to obtain such a Land Act as he desired if he had not known that this was the way to gain for his revolutionary political schemes the support of the small farmers who had refused to countenance the Fenian conspiracy.

He was not mistaken; for, as he well understood, men in general may easily be led away by skilful appeals to their covetous and selfish desires, if such attempts to entice them into wrong are not met from the first by a firm resistance. He knew also that he need not fear having to meet any such resistance from those with whom he had to deal in his endeavour to bring over the Irish peasantry to the cause of Home Rule by hanging out to them as a bait for their support the expectation of obtaining possession of the estates of their landlords. The event has shown how correctly he had judged both his own position, and the character of the government. His policy has proved to have been skilfully contrived for its purposes, and it has been but too successful, thanks to Mr. Gladstone having so completely played into his hands, even at the time that he was locking him up in Kilmainham prison, and denouncing the leaders of the League as "steeped to the lips in treason." That Mr. Gladstone was really playing into his hands, though of course he did not then intend it, is very obvious, if we consider how inevitably the Land Act of 1881 was regarded by the peasant farmers of Ireland as a new and valuable boon won for them by the Land League and by intimidation. They could look upon it in no other light, knowing as they did that it was passed by the authors of the Act of 1870, in flagrant contradiction of the opinions they had most strongly expressed, and of the promises they had given while that measure was in progress, and that this sudden concession was granted just at a time when the agitation carried on by the Land League, and the outrages which, as Mr. Gladstone said, followed its steps, had created general dismay. It is difficult to conceive how any course could have been contrived better calculated to encourage lawlessness, and to increase the power of the Land Leaguers over the minds of the Irish, than that which was thus taken by the government of Mr. Gladstone. And its mischievous effect was probably increased, instead of being diminished, by the imprisonment of Mr. Parnell and some of his associates under the novel and indefensible provisions of Mr. Gladstone's Coercion Act of 1881, which empowered the Lord Lieutenant of Ireland to order the imprisonment for an indefinite time of persons "reasonably suspected" of having been guilty of certain offences.* This imprisonment

* The unjustifiable character of the provisions I refer to in the

was with good reason regarded as unjust by a large part of the Irish population, and consequently tended rather to increase than to diminish the influence over them of those who suffered it, while it was not of such a character as either to deter them from persevering in their opposition to the government and to the law, or seriously to impede them in their hostile action. The passing of the Coercion Act of 1881, and the use made of the powers it conferred on the government, did nothing, therefore, towards averting the evil which was sure to arise from making any fresh concessions to Irish tenants, at the expense of their landlords, in the state of things which existed when the Land Act of the same year was brought forward. The provisions of this Act were even more objectionable than its purpose of making fresh concessions to Irish tenants at a time when it was so specially inexpedient to do so, but I need not now stop to discuss them, as their faults, as well as those of the preceding Act of 1870, of

Act of 1881 does not seem to have attracted the notice it deserves with reference to Mr. Gladstone's denunciation of the Crimes Act of the present year, I therefore add as a note at the end of this essay some remarks I made on this subject in an article I contributed to the "Nineteenth Century Review" for June 1882.

the Arrears Act which followed, and of the policy to which this legislation was meant to give effect, will be best shown by observing what have been their results. In order to understand these results, we have only to compare the state of Ireland before the beginning of the party contest which brought Mr. Gladstone into power at the close of 1868, with what it had become when he resigned the office of prime minister in June 1885. During the whole of these seventeen years, the policy by which Ireland was ruled was that of Mr. Gladstone. His colleagues, of course, share his responsibility, but there is good ground for believing that his ascendancy over them was so great that they followed his lead with little exercise of their own judgment, and some of them, it is commonly supposed, not without reluctance. There is, therefore, no inaccuracy in describing the policy of the government, while he was at its head, as that of Mr. Gladstone himself; and though power was held between 1874 and 1880 by an administration to which he was opposed, this interruption of his ministerial authority did not occasion a change of Irish policy. So far as relates to the executive government, there was not, it is true, under Lord

Beaconsfield, so much want of firmness in discouraging the party of agitation, and in enforcing the law, as under his rival, and in consequence, during the six years of his administration, the state of Ireland was less unsatisfactory than it speedily became when Mr. Gladstone returned to power in 1880. But without legislation, which Lord Beaconsfield did not attempt (whether wisely or unwisely I abstain from enquiring), no real change could be made in Mr. Gladstone's policy, and it remained in continuous operation during the seventeen years I have referred to. The comparison, therefore, which I propose to make will be between the state of Ireland as it was at the beginning, and as it was at the close, of these years, and for this purpose I will only call to mind a few of the facts which are of most importance, as showing the real condition of the country at each of these periods. Of those that relate to 1868, I have already given some account, with the evidence on which it rests; those I shall have to mention respecting 1885 are too well known to require proof.

In 1868 the present farmers were in general on good terms with their landlords; there were exceptions to the rule, but, for the most part, the relations between the two classes were friendly, and on many large estates most cordial; for generations landlords and tenants of the same families had succeeded each other, rents had been regularly paid, and the tenants had been in the habit of going to their landlords or their agents for advice and assistance, which were willingly given, when they required it. In 1885, throughout the greater part of Ireland, tenants had been taught to regard their landlords as enemies, with whom no terms were to be kept, and the bitterest hostility too generally prevailed between them, though in some tenants the old hereditary attachment to the family of their landlord still survived, in spite of all that had been done to destroy it. In 1868 the peasant farmers had given clear proof that they would not give countenance to the seditious designs of the Fenian conspiracy, but, on the contrary, were prepared to support the constituted authorities of the state in maintaining the authority of the law, and did their duty as jurymen fairly and impartially in the trial of persons accused of agrarian as well as of other offences. In 1885, in three provinces, and, I fear, in parts of the fourth, a large proportion both of the peasantry, and of the inhabitants of the towns, belonged to the National League as it was called, against which and its leaders Mr. Gladstone, during the previous years, had thought it necessary largely to use the powers conferred upon him by the very stringent coercion Acts he had called upon Parliament to pass. In 1885 so many of those who were required to serve as jurymen were either themselves members of the League, or too much in dread of it to discharge their duties as they ought, that it was in most places impossible to obtain verdicts, even on the clearest evidence, against persons accused of murders, or other outrages, arising from agrarian agitation. Lawlessness reigned in many districts, and a large proportion of the Queen's most loyal subjects had no security either for the safety of their persons, or the undisturbed enjoyment of their property. In 1868 the practice of "boycotting" was unknown; in 1885 the cruellest tyranny was exercised by means of it over all classes in most parts of Ireland. In 1868, a marked, though not a very rapid, improvement was going on in agriculture, landlords were borrowing large sums of money for draining, building, and other improvements, on their estates; there was no difficulty in obtaining loans for these purposes; some English capital was coming into Ireland for investment in various industrial enterprises, and land commanded so ready a sale that Mr. Maguire stated in his speech that twenty-five or twenty-six, or even up to twenty-seven years' purchase had to be paid for it.* In 1885 the progress of agricultural improvement had been well nigh stopped, no money was being borrowed for draining or other works, and it is said that not uncommonly the mouths of drains, previously made, were no longer kept clear, because landlords had practically been deprived of the power of requiring their tenants to attend to this necessary work. Instead of there being an influx of capital into Ireland to give additional employment to the population, those persons on this side of the channel, who had the misfortune of having money invested on the other, were endeavouring when they could to withdraw it. Land had become absolutely unsaleable, and of money, which had been lent on its security, neither the principal nor the interest could in many cases be obtained. Religious animosities in 1868 were comparatively

* Hansard, vol. cxc., p. 1291.

quiescent; in 1885 their smouldering embers had been fanned into fresh and most mischievous activity, while the Roman Catholic clergy, who in the former period displayed no spirit of hostility to the constituted authorities, were in the latter among the fiercest promoters of political and agrarian agitation, and their Church was being lowered in the eyes of sincere Christians of all denominations by the part many of its priesthood were taking in the support of schemes it is impossible to reconcile with the plainest laws of Christian morals.

I venture to assert that it is impossible to controvert the facts I have now stated as to the contrast between the condition of Ireland before and after it had been brought under the operation of Mr. Gladstone's policy; but no dry statement of facts can give even a faint idea of the amount of distress and unhappiness which have been brought upon all classes of its inhabitants. In order even partly to understand how terrible these have been, and still continue to be, the touching accounts published by some of the sufferers of what they have had to endure ought to be carefully studied. Such was the state of things in Ireland when Mr.

Gladstone resigned office in June 1885, as compared to what it had been in 1868, and it has become worse since he has declared himself a convert to the policy of Home Rule. For this lamentable change he is mainly responsible; much evil has, no doubt, been caused by the seditious agitation of Mr. Parnell and his followers, but I believe they would have been able to do little harm had it not been for the unwise policy towards Ireland, for which Mr. Gladstone has obtained the sanction of Parliament, and for the unjustifiable language, which from 1868 to the present time he has not ceased to use, and which, if it had been intended for that purpose, could not have been more skilfully contrived to excite hatred against the British government and nation, and religious animosities amongst themselves in the the Irish people, and to encourage lawlessness. In a speech he made in Wales last June, Mr. Gladstone described the condition of Ireland as "intolerable," and he told his hearers it was the "effect and fruit" of the manner in which it has been governed. I agree with him that the condition of Ireland well deserved his description of it as "intolerable," and also that this condition is "the effect and fruit" of the manner in which it has been governed. I do not doubt that, as a general rule, the question whether the government of any country has been wisely or unwisely conducted is mainly to be judged by the condition of its people; if they enjoy peace and security, if industry is thriving among them, and if they are not distracted by civil and religious animosities, we may conclude they have been well governed, as we must come to the opposite conclusion if the state of things is the reverse of what I have described. Judged by this test, it is impossible to deny that the government of Ireland has been a bad one. But it is not true that we must look back so far, as Mr. Gladstone would have us, for the bad government which has produced this deplorable result; it is not to be found in what he calls "the depth of the long, painful, and shameful history of the relations between England and Ireland for 700 years." Nineteen years ago Ireland was not in its present "intolerable condition"; on the contrary, by his own admission, which I have quoted, its condition, though by no means altogether satisfactory, was a hopeful and improving one, the worst faults in its government and legislation had been remedied, and if the baleful spirit of party had not interfered, those faults which still remained might also have been easily and safely corrected. But this spirit did interfere, and were it not that I should be led too far from my present purpose, I think I could show that its pernicious influence may be traced in the conduct both of Mr. Gladstone and his followers, and in that of the leaders on the other side. Whether I am right or not in attributing so much evil influence to party spirit, it is, at all events, impossible to controvert my two assertions: first, that from the beginning of 1869 to the middle of 1885, the government of Ireland has been conducted under the guidance of Mr. Gladstone, who has been the author of all the important measures of legislation with regard to it which have been passed by Parliament in those years; and, secondly, that in the course of the same years a most remarkable change for the worse has taken place in the condition of that country. These are plain and undeniable facts, on which the public would do well to ponder at this time, in consequence of the position now taken up by Mr. Gladstone on the Irish question.

Let me call attention to what that position is :

he continues to insist upon the necessity of granting what is called "Home Rule" to Ireland, and to denounce the present ministers, and all who support them on this subject, for refusing this demand, declaring that their doing so is the real obstacle to the restoration of internal peace and order in that country, as if it were something too clear to require proof that this would follow from the establishment of Home Rule, though the great majority of men of education and judgment, not blinded by party feelings, are convinced that it would instead be the means of bringing upon Ireland the miseries of anarchy and of civil war. But while he holds this language he cannot be induced, by any enquiry, however pressing, to give a clear explanation of what he means by " Home Rule." From what he has said and written, I can only gather that he means Ireland to have a separate Parliament and a separate government, to which is to be given, "subject," as he says, " to the unity of the empire and the authority of Parliament, a full and real power to manage exclusively Irish affairs." And in the same speech in which he made this statement (that delivered at Swansea on the 4th of June), he mentions as one of the essential points of his scheme, " that imperial unity should be preserved—of course, through the supremacy of Parliament."

But I do not find that, either in this speech (which was looked for with great interest, as it was understood that it was to contain an exposition of his views), or in that which he made in October at Nottingham, or in his many other speeches and letters, Mr. Gladstone has explained what affairs he considers to be " exclusively Irish." He has no less carefully avoided explaining to what arrangements he proposes to trust for rendering the management of these Irish affairs by the new Irish Parliament and government consistent with " Imperial unity " and the " supremacy of Parliament." On these all-important points the Bill Mr. Gladstone introduced into the House of Commons for carrying his scheme of Home Rule into effect was obscure and unsatisfactory. I will content myself with referring to one out of the many points on which his Bill was most dangerously obscure. Hitherto " Imperial unity " has been understood to imply that the Crown by its ministers, and with the support of Parliament, should have full authority to use the whole power and resources of all the divisions of the United Kingdom for their common defence, and for the promotion of their common interest. But in Mr. Gladstone's Home Rule Bill I am unable to discover any provisions which would sufficiently secure the Imperial Government from being unduly hampered in the exercise of this power in Ireland by the new Irish authorities. Circumstances might arise in which this would be the source of great danger, as, for instance, if there should be reason to apprehend an invasion of Ireland—perhaps by American-Irish buccaneers—or that violence was likely to be attempted against some of Her Majesty's peaceable and loyal subjects in that part of the United Kingdom. In such a case it surely would not be safe that Her Majesty's Ministers should be unable to take any measures of precaution in Ireland they might think necessary, without having to obtain the assent of an Irish Parliament (of which Mr. Parnell would be the probable leader), and of Irish ministers depending on that Parliament for their power.

This is but a single example, out of many it would be easy to mention, of the difficulties which would have been likely to arise under the new constitution the Home Rule Bill of 1886 purposed to create; but it is enough to show how crude and ill-considered the measure was, and how justly it was therefore rejected by the House of Commons, and still more decisively condemned by the nation when it was appealed to by the dissolution of Parliament. So decisive was this condemnation that many of those who were returned at the general election as followers of Mr. Gladstone could only secure their seats by declaring that they would not support his measure in the form in which it had been brought forward, some, I believe, going so far as to say that in this form they regarded it as dead and buried. Even Mr. Gladstone himself, if I can venture to put an interpretation on his many enigmatical sayings, has implied, if he has not distinctly stated, that it will not again be submitted to Parliament in its original shape, if he should again be enabled to force himself into power by the help of his new allies. As to how it is to be altered, however, no information can be obtained; all we are told is that by these alterations certain things are to be accomplished, and especially that, while an Irish Parliament and government are to be created,

"Imperial unity" and the "Supremacy of Parliament" are still to be maintained unimpaired. Most of those who, by their political knowledge, are best qualified to form a judgment on the subject, believe these two things to be incompatible with each other, and that it is impossible that a separate Parliament and Government should be installed in Dublin, with "full and real power to manage exclusively Irish affairs," without depriving the Parliament which sits in Westminster, and the ministers who are responsible to it, of much of the authority and power which are indispensable for the efficient discharge of their duties. This is the opinion entertained by a large majority of those who are styled by Mr. Gladstone the "classes," from whose decision he appeals to the "masses." Will any man of common sense deny that, on a question of this kind, the "classes" are at least as likely as the "masses" to come to a right conclusion? and even if it could be shown that they have failed to do so, and that it may not be so absolutely impossible as they suppose to devise a scheme by which the British and the Irish authorities would be enabled to work together without clashing, and without diminishing the vigour of the Queen's Government over the whole United Kingdom, still it cannot be denied that to contrive such a scheme would be a matter of extreme difficulty, and has not yet been accomplished. Mr. Gladstone has had an opportunity of preparing a plan for this purpose, but that which he produced has been almost universally rejected. I doubt whether there is a single constituency either in England, or even in Scotland, which has shown a disposition to accept it in the form in which it was proposed; and it was very apparent that his Irish allies only supported it as a step to some larger concession.

After so conspicuous a failure, it is surely not a little unreasonable in Mr. Gladstone to ask the nation to replace him in power for the purpose of bringing forward a new measure, on his simple assurance that it will be a better one than the last, and that it will successfully accomplish the different and seemingly inconsistent objects which he assures us it shall answer. This is a demand on the confidence of the nation which no statesman, however high may be his position and his claims to be trusted, is entitled to make. If Mr. Gladstone can suggest a mode of establishing "Home Rule" in Ireland free from the fatal objections to which his measure of 1886 was proved to be open, he ought distinctly to explain at least the heads of this scheme, that it may be submitted to public discussion, before we are called upon to accept so hazardous and so momentous a change in the constitution of our government. In asking the country to declare itself in favour of " Home Rule," without being told what Home Rule is, and to entrust him with power to carry his unknown scheme into effect, Mr. Gladstone is treating the nation much as a nurse treats a child when she says to it, " Open your mouth and shut your eyes, and see what God will send you." The child is rewarded for trusting to its nurse, and doing what it is bid, by having a cherry or a sugar-plum dropped into its mouth. The nation has no right to look for so satisfactory a result, if, trusting to the promises of Mr. Gladstone, it confers upon him the power of carrying a measure of " Home Rule," of which, as yet, we know little, except that we are told it must be satisfactory to Ireland, which, of course, means satisfactory to Mr. Parnell.

When Mr. Gladstone was successfully contending for power in 1868, and afterwards, when he was recommending the measures it enabled him to carry, he promised with unbounded confidence, and in most glowing language, that the policy he persuaded Parliament to sanction would open a new era of peace and prosperity for Ireland, and make its union with this country more real and cordial than it had ever hitherto been. We have seen how miserably delusive these promises have proved, and their failure ought to be a warning to the nation to place no reliance on the similar promise he is now reiterating, with unabated confidence, of the good he will accomplish if the power of granting Home Rule to Ireland is placed in his hands. We may be assured that if, in spite of experience, this power is conferred upon him, the result will be disastrous to the whole United Kingdom, and more especially to Ireland. In giving an account of the character and results of Mr. Gladstone's Irish policy, and more especially of his legislation respecting land, I have been chiefly anxious to impress this warning on the public, as being what is most important at the present moment. But there remains to be considered another question, still more important for the future, as to what measures can be taken with the greatest prospect of success for the restoration of Ireland from the "intolerable condition" it has been brought into by the system of government and of legislation of recent years. To this question I will address myself in the next chapter.

CHAPTER V.

WHAT MEASURES ARE NOW REQUIRED FOR IRELAND?

BEFORE I enter upon the enquiry which is to form the subject of this chapter, I feel bound to offer an apology for venturing (as I shall have to do) to declare opinions greatly at variance with those hitherto expressed by the leaders of all political parties upon a subject of such extreme difficulty, as well as importance, and also to suggest the adoption of a course which will probably be regarded as of too violent a character for serious consideration. My excuse for this apparent presumption is that for upwards of sixty years, as a member, first of the House of Commons, and afterwards of the House of Lords, I have watched with close attention, and not unfrequently taken part in, the proceedings of

Parliament with reference to Ireland, that I have always felt a very deep interest in its welfare, and that its situation appears to me to have now become so critical that some great calamity must soon ensue unless very decided steps are promptly taken to avert the danger. I am further convinced that the evils that afflict Ireland would be aggravated instead of being relieved by some, at least, of the measures proposed for their remedy, and that none have yet been suggested which could reasonably be expected to prove sufficient to meet the difficulties of the present time. In these circumstances, though I am well aware how much risk I incur of bringing upon myself both blame and ridicule as a visionary schemer, I think it my duty to submit to the public, without reserve, the conclusions I have arrived at, after long and anxious consideration, as to the course which would be most likely to bring the nation safely through the perils that surround it.

The question as to what it would be expedient to do in legislating for Ireland will be much simplified by first considering what ought to be avoided; and on this point I would call attention to the hopelessness of any legislation proving beneficial to the people if its aim is still to be merely to gratify their wishes, instead of to promote their real welfare by wise and just measures. If my memory does not deceive me, Mr. Gladstone, soon after he took up Irish policy as the ground for his attack on a Conservative administration, laid it down, as a rule to be followed, that Parliament, in legislating for Ireland, ought to be guided by the wishes of the Irish people. I am unable to refer to the speech in which this opinion was expressed, but I am pretty sure I am right as to the substance of what he said, and, at all events, it seems sufficiently clear, from his measures, that the rule, I believe him to have distinctly laid down in words, has been that on which, so far as he was able, he practically acted in his Irish legislation while the government was in his hands. I venture very confidently to assert that this is not the way in which legislation, either for Ireland or for the rest of the United Kingdom, ought to be conducted. In deciding what laws are to be passed, it is the duty of Parliament, and of the ministers to whom for the time it trusts for advice, to be guided by what, after careful consideration, is judged to be best for the whole community, and not by the mere wishes of any part of the population, however strongly they may be expressed. For it by no means follows that because laws are clamorously demanded they must be good ones; they cannot be good, and must undoubtedly fail to promote the true welfare of those for whose benefit they are intended, if they are not in strict conformity with justice, and also in accordance with those economic laws to which human society has been made subject by an all-wise Providence. Men's passions, their selfish covetousness, and, still more commonly, their ignorance, often lead them to call upon their rulers for legislation which, judged by this test, deserves to be condemned; in such cases it is the part of wise and honest statesmen not to plead the wishes of the people as a reason for doing what is wrong, but to use their utmost efforts, and all the influence they can command, in resisting measures which are calculated to prove hurtful to the nation.

I have made these observations, because the legislation as to Irish land, which I have described in the last chapter, seems to me to bear plain marks of having been far too much influenced by the desire to obtain the favour of the small farmers who now exercise a predominant power in Irish elections, and too little by a regard for sound principles of legislation. With regard to these principles, we were even told that the rules of political economy might be good for the inhabitants of Jupiter or of Saturn, but that those who would apply them in Ireland ought to be treated as dreamers. Notwithstanding this scoff, experience has proved in this, as in so many other cases, that those great economic laws which are known as the rules of political economy can never be violated by any nation with impunity, and sooner or later every such violation brings upon the country which is guilty of it its proper punishment in the shape of the evil consequences that follow. To recognise this truth, and to resolve to act upon it, would be the first step towards bringing about a better state of things in Ireland, and I most deeply deplore that the present government, instead of doing this, is following the example of Mr. Gladstone's former administrations. The Land Act of 1887 is another step in the way which was entered upon by the Acts of 1870 and 1881. Again, by this new Act, as by the former ones, resistance to the law has been rewarded by fresh concessions to those who have been guilty of it, and the "plan of campaign," and the use of hot lime and scalding water against men for doing their duty in carrying the law into effect, have gained for the class by which these things have been done the power of obtaining a further deduction from what was left to landlords of their property by former measures, and a new proof has been given how little reliance can be placed on the stability of legislation deliberately sanctioned by Parliament, and on contracts made under its authority. But the Act is passed, and cannot now be altered; it is not therefore worth while to go further in trying to show its faults, numerous and glaring as they are ; I cannot, however, omit to mention that I think the evil effects to be expected from it, are likely to be not a little increased by the reasons assigned for bringing it forward. If I rightly understand what was said on behalf of the government, it really came to this, that, while they could not deny the principle on which the Bill is founded to be unsound, they argued that this erroneous principle had been so far admitted by past legislation that it was necessary to go further in the same direction, because the state of things which had been created was one which could not be allowed to continue. The danger of acting on this view of the subject is obvious; it holds out to us the prospect of a course of legislation, going from bad to worse, till it ends in utter confusion.

The unsatisfactory, or rather exceedingly dangerous, state of the relations between the owners and the occupiers of land in Ireland, which has grown up under the operation of Mr. Gladstone's Land Acts, is not to be denied; but it is contrary to common sense to contend that a recognition of this fact affords a reason for consenting to further measures founded on the same vicious policy, which has produced the evils that have become so formidable. The conclusion to which we ought to be led by a careful consideration of the Land Acts already passed, and of their effects, is that a firm stand ought at length to be taken against all further legislation not based on those principles which have been recognized as sound by the wisest statesmen and political writers. This is not, I fear, the view at present taken of the subject by the majority of politicians, to whatever party they belong. They feel so strongly the evils of the existing disorganisation of society in Ireland that they seem willing to give their assent to almost any plausible scheme for remedying these evils, without a sufficiently careful study of what are likely to be the real results of the measures recommended for adoption. Among these schemes that which seems to be the most popular is one for getting rid of what is called "dual property in land," by enabling the tenants, by some means or other, to acquire the absolute ownership of the farms they hold. It is not yet known whether Her Majesty's Ministers contemplate proposing any measure for this purpose in the ensuing Session, and in spite of some ominous expressions of opinion that fell from them in the last, I trust that, when they give to the subject the careful consideration it will require before they come to a practical decision, they will see that the objections to any such proposal are insuperable. For my own part, I am entirely unable to understand how it is possible that they can come to a different conclusion. Even if there were no other obstacle to the adoption of a project for converting a large proportion of the Irish tenantry into owners of the farms they hold, one which could not be overcome would arise from the necessity of providing the very large sum of money which would be required to carry the scheme into effect.

We may presume that no British government would ever sanction so outrageous a measure of confiscation as depriving the landlords of Ireland of their property without giving them full compensation, and the sum of money required for that purpose must be a very large one. It was estimated by Mr. Gladstone, if I am not mistaken, at a hundred and thirteen millions, but there appear to be good grounds for believing that this would fall considerably short of the amount which would be necessary in order to meet the just claims of those who would be deprived of their property. It would, however, be a waste of labour to try to calculate what sum of money would have to be provided for the purchase of the rights of Irish proprietors to their lands, since the lowest estimate of what would be wanted far exceeds what Parliament would be justified in appropriating for such a purpose. For it must be borne in mind (though the fact seems to be generally forgotten) that the effect of any one of the various schemes that have been proposed would be to reward the Irish tenantry for their lawlessness, and their refusal to pay the rents they owe, by giving them, at the expense of the British taxpayers, possession as owners of land they now only hold as tenants. Those who contend for the adoption of a scheme of this kind will, of course, deny that any burthen would be thereby thrown on British taxpayers; they admit that the help of the national credit would be necessary, but they assert that no demand need be made on the British treasury to carry into effect the proposed change in the ownership of Irish land. They assert that ample provision might be made for the interest and the sinking fund on the loan it would be necessary to raise for the compensation of the present landowners, by very moderate annuities, to be charged on the land, and paid by the tenants, who are to become its proprietors. I do not dispute that annuities, which might fairly be called moderate as compared to the value of the land, would be sufficient, if regularly paid, to meet the charge for interest and sinking fund on a loan large enough to pay to Irish landlords a compensation for the surrender of their property, which in the present state of things they might not be unwilling to accept, though less than they might justly demand. But the question whether the regular payment of the annuities could be relied upon does not seem to have received the attention it deserves, considering the difficulties that must be expected to arise in collecting them. Although the annuity it is proposed that the farmer should pay in order ultimately to become the owner of his land would be considerably less than his present rent, I can see nothing to justify an expectation that it would be regularly paid. The very fact of such an enormous boon being offered to him, since the "plan of campaign" has been put in operation, would be regarded as a new proof that he and his fellows are able by combination to defeat the law, and he is not likely to forget the lesson he has been so carefully taught, that he ought to be allowed his land without paying anything for it. It is as little likely that he will be more ready to part with his money to pay his debt to what he regards as a hostile government than he has lately been to pay his rent to his landlord. We have no right, therefore, to expect that the annuities will be willingly paid by the great majority of those by whom they will be due, and to collect them from unwilling debtors holding the land in small allotments will be a matter of extreme difficulty.

To whom is this difficult duty of collection to be entrusted? No local authority would be likely to perform it efficiently, and the objections to imposing such a task on the servants of the government are obvious; it would require almost an army of collectors to levy the amount due in small sums from the many thousands of farmers who would be chargeable. Then there would be frequent applications for time to be allowed before payment was insisted upon from men, who would give all sorts of reasons, some good and some bad, for not being able to pay what they owed without some indulgence, and it would require better and more trustworthy agents than would easily be found to decide in what cases indulgence should be granted, and when it should be refused, and on the steps to be taken when payment could not be obtained without having recourse to some compulsory process. In the last resort eviction would, in the case of annuities, be the only means, as it is now with regard to rents, by which payment of their debts by unwilling or insolvent debtors could be enforced, when it could not be obtained by distress, and it can hardly be necessary to point out how much inconvenience, and even danger, would result from its becoming necessary for the government to have recourse to legal proceedings, leading to levies of distress, or to eviction, perhaps, against hundreds or even thousands of peasant farmers. But this is what would surely happen to some extent even in good years, and very largely in bad ones, when the failure of their crops or unusually low prices made it difficult for the new owners of the land to pay the annuities with which they would be charged.*

The difficulties I have only partly described, and the heavy cost of collection would from the first lead to a very large difference between the total amount due to the State by the tenants who had

* I am aware that, in defending the scheme I have been discussing, its advocates point in its favour to the fact that the Church lessees who have purchased the property they held as tenants have met their obligations with great regularity, and that the whole amount due is annually paid by them with a very small per-centage of loss by default. This I believe to be true; but it must be remembered that the Church lessees were, as a class, much superior to the general body of small Irish farmers, and that the circumstances in which they came into possession of their land were so different from those which now exist, that the very limited experiment made in their case affords little ground for anticipating equal success for a similar experiment on the gigantic scale that has been recommended.

become owners of their farms, and the net sum actually paid into the Exchequer to meet the interest on the loan, for which the Treasury would be bound to provide. No reliance, therefore, can be placed in any assurances that may be given that Parliament might authorise the raising of a loan, to compensate Irish landowners for the surrender of their property, without imposing any charge on the country. It is mere delusion to suppose that this could be done, and the fact ought to be recognised that to use the national credit in any form in aid of a scheme for buying up the property of Irish landlords for the benefit of the tenants, must end in throwing a heavy burden on British taxpayers.

In the preceding remarks I have confined my attention to the pecuniary objections there are to the scheme of purchasing the land of Irish proprietors on a large scale, which has obtained so much support, but I cannot leave the subject without expressing my strong conviction that, even if the money difficulty could be overcome, a greater calamity could hardly be inflicted upon Ireland than carrying this scheme into effect. I have already expressed my concurrence in Mr.

Parnell's opinion, that the landlords of Ireland form its English garrison, and to those, who believe with myself that to maintain the Union is indispensable for the welfare of both islands, the policy of destroying this " garrison," which is the most powerful support of Imperial authority, must appear exceedingly unwise. And this is not all; the landlords are not only an invaluable support to Imperial authority, but they are also the most efficient instruments for the civilisation and improvement of the Irish people. The fact seems to be lost sight of that, speaking of the country generally, and making an exception for some districts, and for the principal towns, the population is in a very low state of civilization. If left to themselves there is little prospect that they would rise to a higher condition, but the Irish people have many admirable qualities, and, if well managed and wisely guided, are capable of forming a society enjoying all that is required for the welfare and the advancement of mankind. For this purpose two things are wanted ; first, discipline, and the creation of a sense of the necessity of obedience to the law ; and next, instruction, by example, rather than by precept, in the habits and practices of civilised life, and in the arts of industry. In both these ways the presence of the landlords is of inestimable value to Ireland, and especially, as I have already shown, in the work of agricultural improvement. Without the aid of a large body of intelligent and educated men having themselves an interest in this work, there would be little probability of improvement being carried on.

It is not only an absence of improvement we should have to fear, but a deterioration in the condition of the people, if the idea could be realised of getting rid of a majority at least of the class of landlords, and the conversion of peasant farmers into proprietors. If this should be accomplished it is probable that the peasant proprietors would act very much in the same way as they usually did as farmers, when they were allowed to follow their own inclinations. We should expect, therefore, that they would very often put up cabins for sons and sons-in-law, or for labourers to whom they would let portions of their land. It is well known that a large proportion of Irish small farmers are in the habit of endeavouring to do this, and often with success, in spite of the law against sub-letting, on ill-managed properties. On well-managed estates vigilance on the part of the landlord or his agent prevents the land from being thus dealt with. But with the peasant farmers, when they have become owners of their land, no one will have a right to interfere, nor would it be practically possible to impose by law any effectual restrictions on their power to do what they liked with their land, so that, in the manner I have described, and by the division of farms, on the death of the original proprietors, among their children, there is the strongest probability that in a few years the freeholds it is desired to create would be cut up into small allotments insufficient to maintain the holders in decent comfort. The land would thus become covered by as large a population as could obtain from it even a miserable subsistence, and living in a state of wretchedness and degradation. We must also expect that like small landowners in all countries in which they form a considerable class, and notably in France, and in India, the Irish landowners would soon be weighed down by the debts they would incur to money-lenders.

Perhaps I shall be asked by what means the land question is to be settled if we are to reject the scheme of converting the small tenants into proprietors by purchasing the rights of the present landowners. It may be said that the conditions under which land is now held in Ireland are hopelessly bad; that the landlord, under the existing land laws, has so little control over the land of which he is still the legal owner, that he cannot be expected to spend any money on its improvement, while the tenant, though he has a right of occupation, has not the same motives to improvement which he would have if the land belonged to him. This "dual ownership," as it has been called, is thus an obstacle to improvement, and tends to create hostility between landlords and tenants. Such appear to be the reasons which have led many persons to the conclusion that another attempt ought to be made to reform the land laws of Ireland, and to improve the position of the cultivators of the soil. I am far from denying that there is much truth in what is said as to the evils arising from the present system of land tenure. I do not doubt that the "dual ownership" of land is exceedingly unsatisfactory, and works badly both for landlords and tenants, but when we come to consider how the evil, which has been done by the unwise legislation of 1870 and 1881, can be cured, I fear we shall be forced to admit that the greater part of it is now irremediable. It is impossible, as I have endeavoured to show, to alter the position of the occupiers of land by converting them into proprietors, and on the other hand, however unwise the Land Acts of 1870 and 1881 may have been, to repeal them now would be as great a mistake as it was to pass them. It would give a new proof of the instability of purpose, which has been one of the worst faults of Parliament, and of the fact that the maintenance of rights it has recognised or granted is not to be relied upon. I hold, therefore, that the existing state of things ought to be maintained, so far as refusing to make any further alteration of the law in favour either of landlords or of tenants. Two things only occur to me as practicable for the purpose of mitigating the evils which have been caused by the unwise legislation respecting land which Parliament has been induced to sanction. In the first place, it ought to be distinctly announced that no further attempt will be made to relieve Irish tenants by again altering by law the terms on which they hold their land, and that for the future they will be required strictly to perform the engagements by which they are bound. Secondly, power might be given to landlords and tenants, when both concurred in desiring it, to relieve the land held by tenants from the inconvenient and complicated system of tenure created by the Land Acts of 1870 and 1881, in order that it might be held by agreement on terms freely arranged between the parties concerned. An Act might be passed enabling these parties, when they both desired it, to enter into contracts as to the occupation of land, unfettered by the existing Land Acts, and giving facilities for making and recording agreements for this purpose, by means of a law framed on the principle of the Bill approved in 1868 by the Committee of the House of Lords.

I do not offer these suggestions from any belief that the evils Ireland is now suffering could be cured by adopting them. These evils are in my opinion the natural fruits of unwise legislation, and of inefficient administration of the executive government during many years, and do not admit of a speedy remedy. The most to be hoped for from anything that could now be done, would be to check the operation of the causes which are now tending to increase the existing evils, and to give facilities for the gradual, though it must be a slow, restoration of a more healthy state of society. In both these ways I venture to think the course I have suggested would be useful. One of the worst results of Mr. Gladstone's legislation as to land, and of his entire abandonment in 1881 of principles, which in 1870 he had represented as of vital importance, has been that all feeling of security as to the permanence of the existing law, and as to the maintenance of the rights which that law confers, has been destroyed. While this sense of insecurity continues, it is vain to look for agricultural or industrial improvement on the scale the country requires, or to expect the tenantry to settle down to the steady work of cultivating their farms instead of joining in political agitation in the hope of obtaining some additional share of their landlord's property. Hence it is of the very highest importance that it should be made clear to the population that there will be no more tinkering of the land laws for the purpose of conferring fresh advantages on the tenants at the expense of their landlords, and that the performance of their contracts, both by landlords and by tenants, will be enforced in accordance with Mr. Gladstone's declaration in 1870, that, from the moment his measure of that year was passed, "every Irishman, small or great, must be absolutely responsible for every contract into which he enters."

I am aware that there will be much difficulty in refusing fresh concessions, and still more in enforcing the payment by tenants of even the reduced rents they are still bound to pay, the cry raised against what are asserted to be the excessive rents demanded for land in Ireland, and against the alleged cruelty of evictions, has been too successful among English members of the House of Commons. Severe pressure is likely in consequence to be brought to bear on Her Majesty's Ministers to induce them to propose to Parliament some further concessions in favour of Irish tenants, and to abstain from giving that firm and uncompromising support to the officers of the law in carrying its processes into effect, which they have a right to look for. There is reason to fear that some, and perhaps not a very small number, even of those members of the House of Commons who usually support the government, may oppose the policy of maintaining the law as it stands, and of resolutely enforcing obedience to it, on the ground that rents are too high, and are justly denounced by the followers of Mr. Parnell as "impossible." Yet there is no proof whatever that Irish rents have been unduly high, but, on the contrary, much evidence the other way. Mr. Gladstone, in proposing his Land Bill of 1881, said "that it was unusual in Ireland to exact what in England would have been considered a full and fair commercial rent," and among persons well skilled in agriculture, both English and foreign, who have visited Ireland for the purpose of forming a judgment as to its real condition, there has been a general concurrence of opinion that, as a rule, the rents paid in Ireland are considerably lower than those which are charged in England for land of similar quality. A more conclusive proof that land is not let at extravagant rents in Ireland is to be found in the fact that the tenant-right of farms habitually sells at a high price. It is obvious that, when a new tenant pays to the previous holder of a farm a large sum for the right of succeeding him as its occupier at the same rent, this implies that the new tenant must consider the farm to be worth not only the rent due to the landlord, but also what is equivalent to an additional rent in the shape of interest on the money paid for tenant-right. From the accounts of sales of tenant-right, which appear from time to time in the newspapers, we learn that large sums are constantly paid for tenant-right; in some cases it is stated that the tenant-right has been sold at a higher price than the property still left to the landlord would bring. If I am not misinformed, even in the counties where the resistance to the payment of rents has been most determined, and in this time of agricultural depression, there are few if any farms of which the tenants could not, if they wished it, get a substantial price for their tenant-right.

If this is so, it follows that Irish rents are not usually too high, since tenants are almost always to be found willing to pay more for any farms that are to be had than the rents due to the landlords. I may also remark (though it is scarcely necessary to do so) that, in judging whether the rent payable to a landlord is reasonable or otherwise, no account can be taken of what the tenant has to pay in addition to his rent as interest on the money he has given to a previous occupier for his tenant-right. The actual holder of a farm may have made a bad bargain with the tenant who held it before him, but the landlord is in no way responsible for his having done so, nor does his having made such a bad bargain confer upon the tenant the slightest claim for a reduction of rent. Perhaps it may be said that rents were not too high a few years ago, but that the great fall of prices has rendered it impossible that they should now be paid without large reductions. In reply, it may be observed that very large reductions of rent have been made or offered by almost all Irish landlords to tenants willing to pay just and reasonable demands upon them. In Ireland, also, there is, as in England and Scotland, a practical security against landlords insisting upon higher rents than their farms are fairly worth, because, if they do, the farms are thrown upon their hands, and cannot be re-let without loss. There is, therefore, no need for again calling in the assistance of the state for the regulation of rents, and we ought to be warned against doing so by the results of the Act of 1881. The inquiry into the operation of that Act by the House of Lords Committee has so clearly demonstrated the great amount of injustice that was done by decreeing judicial rents, that there would be no excuse for repeating the mistake committed in thus endeavouring to determine rents by authority.

I have mentioned that there is reason to apprehend that objection may be taken to the action of the government if it should resolutely use its power to support those charged with the duty of carrying into effect the decrees of the courts of law. Some persons seem to imagine that when individuals make what is considered a harsh use of their legal rights, and when, in consequence, resistance is offered to the execution of the legal processes by which these rights are to be enforced, the government is justified in withholding its effectual aid for overcoming this resistance. This opinion is held more especially with regard to evictions, and the government has been sometimes greatly blamed for employing the force at its disposal to support the sheriff and his officers in carrying into effect what are called cruel evictions. A very little consideration will be sufficient to show that this is a mistaken view of the subject. Eviction is, in the last resort, the only mode of enforcing legal claims on the occupiers of land, whether these claims are made by landlords against their tenants, or by mortgagees against the owners of land. It is the duty of the legislature to settle by law in what cases a right to evict shall be given, and to do this in such a manner as to guard against injustice in the exercise of the right. I believe that no fault can fairly be found with the existing law of Ireland as sanctioning unjust evictions, but if there is any such fault in the law it is for Parliament to correct it; while the law continues what it is, whenever it is shown that the right to evict has been created by the default of a holder of land to meet his legal obligations, the proper court of law is bound, on the application of the person entitled to ask for eviction, to issue the necessary process for carrying it into effect. The court has no right to exercise any discretion on the subject ; its duty is simply to ascertain whether the person who applies to it is, or is not, entitled to obtain the process he asks for, and, if he is, to issue it as a matter of course. And if this process is resisted, it then becomes the duty of the executive government to use all its power to put down such resistance, and vindicate the authority of the law. Neither the court of law to which application has been made, nor the executive government, has the smallest right to refuse its assistance to a claimant on the ground that he is acting harshly in pressing his legal claims. A landlord may be acting harshly, and in a manner which would expose him to just reproach, but other creditors may also be guilty of cruelty in pressing their claims in certain circumstances, and it would be a direct violation of the most elementary principles of constitutional, or even of any regular, government, if the courts of law were to claim the power of refusing to any man the means of enforcing his legal rights because they appeared to be harshly exercised. The duty of the executive government is no less clear in this matter than that of the courts of law; it is not entitled to assume an arbitrary power of declining to use the force at its disposal to put down resistance to the law, because it disapproves of the conduct of those who have put the law in motion; it is bound in all cases to maintain the authority of the law, and to protect those who are charged with its execution. There is reason to believe that this plain duty of the government has not

always been practically recognised in Ireland, and
that the formidable height, to which the spirit
of lawlessness has now reached there, is mainly
due to the fact that its first displays were not
met with sufficient promptness and determination.

The land question is so justly considered to be
the main difficulty to be dealt with in trying to
raise Ireland from its present unhappy condition,
that the policy on the subject I have ventured to
recommend in the preceding paragraphs will probably be regarded as unsatisfactory. The position
in which tenants now stand towards their landlords must be admitted to be an exceedingly bad
one, and, this being the case, it seems at first sight
natural to conclude that some distinct measure for
improving it ought to be adopted, and that we
ought not to be satisfied with a policy which
would substantially consist in abstaining from any
further alteration of the law which now determines the respective rights of landlords and
tenants, and in firmly enforcing these rights as so
determined. But, on the other hand, it is a fact
which ought not to be lost sight of, that no new
change of the existing law relating to the tenure
of land could be attempted without raising difficult

questions as to how far rights conferred by recent legislation can justly be interfered with, and whether any redress is due to those whose rights have been improperly invaded. Attempting a further change would have the additional inconvenience of tending to check the growing up of confidence in the permanence of any new law which Parliament might enact, or of that now in force, on this difficult subject. The recurrence of changes in laws affecting rights of property is always attended with inconvenience, irrespective of the nature of these changes, from the apprehension they excite as to what may follow. No small part of the evils caused by the Land Act of 1881 arose from its reversing, on various important points, the provisions deliberately adopted in the previous Act of 1870, and thus proving that, in legislating on this question so deeply affecting the welfare of the Irish people, Parliament had not been guided by any well-considered principles or fixity of purpose.

The above reasons for not disturbing the arrangement made in 1881, objectionable as it was, and mischievous as its operation has proved, do not apply to the proposal that an Act should be passed giving power to the parties concerned to revert, in cases where they think fit to do so, to the simple principle of contract for regulating the terms on which land is to be held, with provisions also for giving facilities, which do not now exist, for making and registering agreements for that purpose. It is by no means improbable that after a time this power might be somewhat extensively used by farmers in order to obtain assistance from their landlords, which they could not otherwise expect, in improving their land. Even if the small holders, for whose benefit the Acts of 1870 and 1881 were designed, should not be inclined to give up any advantages they may hope to derive from these Acts, for the sake of the benefit they might obtain by making new agreements with their landlords, there can be no doubt that a boon would be conferred on the larger farmers by affording them greater facilities than they now enjoy for entering into agreements with their landlords, and for having these agreements registered so as to obviate the risk of subsequent dispute. I must add that, while I by no means despair that by degrees a better state of the relations between different classes of the

population of Ireland may be restored, if, for the
future, no attempts are made to relieve by unsound legislation any one class at the expense of
others from difficulties it may have to contend
with, and if order and security can be established,
still I fear many years must go by before the evils
that have been brought upon the country by the
policy pursued since the close of 1868 can be
repaired. We must also expect that the grievous
distress now prevailing among the owners and
occupiers of land on this side of the Irish Channel
will, from the same causes, be felt also on the
other, and probably still more severely. English
and Scotch farmers have generally been able to do
something towards meeting the great fall in the
price of agricultural produce, by the greater use of
machinery and of improved implements, and by
changes in their system of cultivation, to make it
less costly and more productive; but it is much
less easy for Irish farmers, with their generally
small holdings, to meet the pressure of bad times
in this manner. Many Irish farmers are likely to
find the competition, both of foreign produce, and
of that raised in England and Scotland by agriculturists of greater skill and placed in more favour-

able circumstances, too severe for them to encounter with success. Possibly, however, this may not in the end prove to be a misfortune; it may bring about a gradual consolidation of the smallest farms, and thus render it practicable to adopt better means of cultivation, and may also drive a part of the population to seek their livelihood in other branches of industry.

Having thus explained (most imperfectly as I am aware) how I think the land question ought to be dealt with, I will now proceed to consider one or two other suggestions which have been offered for improving the condition of Ireland, and I will begin by saying a few words on the subject of emigration. Many persons insist strongly on the expediency of looking to emigration as one of the most valuable means of affording relief to distress in Ireland, and especially in what are called the congested districts. I do not doubt the importance of emigration as a resource for those who are unable to find the means of earning a fairly good livelihood at home, but I also have the strongest conviction that much evil would result from attempting to promote it by sending out emigrants at the cost of the State. The government can do much to promote successful emigration by enforcing proper regulations to prevent abuses and the neglect of sanitary precautions on board of emigrant ships, and also by inducing the colonial authorities to assist emigrants, who go to any part of the British dominions, by information and advice. But if it attempts to go further than this, and defray the cost of sending out emigrants, very mischievous results will follow, and the amount of emigration that takes place will be diminished instead of being increased. This was the conclusion come to, after much anxious consideration, by the government of Lord John Russell at the time of the Irish famine caused by the potatoe disease. During that great calamity, emigration on a large scale from Ireland was far more needed than it is at present, and the success of the policy then pursued affords a strong argument against now adopting an opposite one. Some account of the reasons which induced the Cabinet of that day to decide against applying to Parliament for any grant of money for carrying out emigrants, and of the good results of the course which was taken, will be found at the end of this essay in an extract from an article I contributed to the "Nineteenth Century Review" for September 1883.*

I have now to turn to another and a very important matter. Two or three years ago some conspicuous opponents of Mr. Parnell's project of Home Rule qualified their opposition to it by expressing their willingness to consider any reasonable plan for giving greater powers of local self-government to the Irish people. Lately we have heard less of this notion, but I fear it has not been abandoned, and it appears to me to be one so full of danger that I must offer some remarks upon it. And, in the first place, I must point out that the Irish people have already very large powers of local government. The grand juries, the municipalities, the boards of guardians, and of commissioners for the improvement of harbours, have ample authority for the management of local concerns: The organisation of local authorities is certainly not less complete in Ireland than in England. These bodies may or may not require reform; that is a question on which I have no wish to express an opinion, but there is no doubt of the fact that they are local bodies, formed on the same principle as the similar bodies in this country, and exercising

* See note B. at the end.

functions of the same description. Such being the case, I am at a loss to understand what is meant, when it is asserted, as it so often is, that a greater power of self-government in local affairs ought to be given to the Irish people. If it only means that a more popular character ought to be given to the existing authorities, I see no objection to the demand being at least fairly considered with the view of making any change which, on due inquiry, may be found expedient, though, looking to the accounts which are published of the proceedings in some town councils and boards of guardians, it may well be doubted whether for the present, at all events, it would be advisable to meet the demand for greater power of local self-government by giving a more popular character to these bodies. This, however, is probably not what is intended by the very vague demand I have referred to. Those by whom it is put forward rather contemplate, so far as I can understand their language, the creation of some kind of representative council exercising a limited control over the local affairs of Ireland generally, or else (as apparently others would prefer) separate councils for each of its four provinces.

If this is really what is meant, it is difficult to understand how those, who regard Mr. Parnell's scheme of Home Rule as one that ought to be strenuously resisted, can look favourably on any project for creating either a single representative council for all Ireland, or four separate ones for the provinces into which it is divided. A single council for all Ireland (and the same remark would apply, though with less force, to provincial councils), in the present state of mind of a great part of the Irish people, would assuredly become a most dangerous obstruction to the action of the executive government. It would be in vain strictly to limit the powers of such a council; it would follow the example of the town councils of Dublin and some other towns, and of some boards of guardians, by passing resolutions condemning the acts of the government, and giving its support by all the means in its power to the revolutionary designs of the followers of Mr. Parnell. But without dwelling on this point, though there is so much to be said upon it, I would observe that I have never yet heard any intelligible statement as to what is to be the business entrusted to a new authority for the management of local affairs. In order to

give this new authority anything to do, some of
the business now managed by the various strictly
local bodies I have mentioned must be withdrawn
from them, or else Parliament must make over to
this new authority some of the functions it has
hitherto kept in its own hands. But to withdraw
from town councils, boards of guardians, and other
similar bodies, any of their duties for the purpose
of transferring them to some more central authority, would be the very reverse of extending the
system of local self-government, and would be a
change greatly for the worse. With regard to
Parliament, I am not aware that any of its functions but one (which I shall presently consider)
could with advantage be given up by it, and committed to a different authority. Its two important
duties of legislation, and of control over the public
purse, could not, as it seems to me, be divided
without manifest inconvenience and damage to
the public interest. The laws which regulate
men's relations with each other in private life
ought to be as nearly as possible the same in the
three divisions of the United Kingdom. If I am
not misinformed, much inconvenience is experienced in the United States from the diversity

of the laws of the different states on some important subjects, especially as to marriage and divorce. We have some experience of this inconvenience with regard to the law of marriage and divorce in the United Kingdom, and the diversity of the law in its different divisions has caused much injustice and very cruel hardship to innocent persons. But with this exception, I am not aware that there is any matter on which differences in the laws are now a source of serious inconvenience in any part of the United Kingdom. For nearly two centuries statesmen and lawyers have been endeavouring gradually to assimilate the laws of England and of Scotland, and in new legislation the same laws are as a general rule made applicable to both. Any division of the legislative authority which is now vested in the Imperial Parliament is therefore, in my opinion, highly inexpedient. A division of the authority now exercised by Parliament in matters of finance, and the establishment of separate national treasuries for England, Scotland, and Ireland, would be even more to be deprecated; but the objections to any scheme of that kind are so obvious that it would be a waste of time to describe them.

I have said that there is one part of the duties of Parliament which I think it might, with advantage, make over to another authority; I refer to what is called its "private business." Very soon after I became a member of the House of Commons, now more than sixty years ago, I formed the opinion, which I have never since abandoned, though I was never able to obtain any substantial support for it, that the manner in which this part of the duties of Parliament is discharged is so unsatisfactory that it ought to be altered. It has been much more unsatisfactory in the House of Commons than in the Lords, for the Upper House has been content to leave a large discretionary power, which has been a great check upon abuses, in the hands of its successive chairmen of committees, and this power has in general been well exercised, though it must be confessed sometimes rather arbitrarily. In the earlier part of my parliamentary life the manner in which private business was managed in the House of Commons was nothing short of a scandal. The committees on private bills were not constituted in such a manner as to entitle them to public confidence, and their decisions were not accepted, as they now have been for many years, as practically binding upon the House except in special cases. The consequence was that the House itself was often called upon to decide on the passing or rejection of private bills on which very large pecuniary interests were at stake, and, as it was impossible that more than a very few members should have any real knowledge of the merits of projects for public works and other measures which require to be authorised by private bills, votes for or against them were chiefly determined by canvass and solicitation, which were carried on with extreme eagerness. I remember when one of the bills relating to the Aire and Calder Navigation was before the House, and it was supposed that the gain of advantages of very great money value by one or other of two contending parties depended on its passing, there was as energetic a "whip," and as large an attendance of members, at the meeting of the House, as if some great political question were going to be decided. In the previous solicitation for votes every kind of influence had been used, without stint, by both parties.

The worst of the old abuses have been got rid of by successive changes that have been made by both Houses in their mode of conducting the business of private legislation, and especially by the system of referring contested bills to small select committees with specially chosen chairmen. Still, the reform that has been accomplished is very far from being complete; the present system, though a great improvement on what formerly existed, still fails to provide that questions of so much difficulty, as well as of such extreme national importance, as some of those that come before committees on bills relating to railways and public works, shall be submitted for the decision of a really competent authority. The knowledge required for forming a sound judgment on these questions is of such a kind that the majority of members of either House can hardly be expected to possess it. Parliamentary committees on private bills, are therefore necessarily unequal to the duty imposed on them, and the more so owing to the manner in which they are constituted. These committees, it must be remembered, are only formed to consider a particular bill, or group of bills, which is referred to them. When they have finished the work thus assigned to them the committees are dissolved, and thus the knowledge and experience gained by their members are, in a great measure, lost for the future. The country thus loses the advantage it would derive from having the very important branch of its business relating to railways conducted by men who gain experience in performing it by regular and constant practice. Another very inconvenient consequence of the want of a permanent authority to deal with this business is that it deprives the measures sanctioned by Parliament of the consistency required for their success. If a bill is brought before Parliament to carry forward some general scheme of which the commencement may have been sanctioned perhaps after a long and costly contest, it rarely, if ever, happens that a committee composed of the same members is called upon to decide whether the steps necessary to complete the original design shall be sanctioned. In general, the new committee consists of members who are entirely ignorant of the views of the former one, and of its reasons for the conclusion it may have come to. Hence it is by no means uncommon for a committee of one year practically to reverse the decision of a former one, sometimes without even being aware that it is doing so.

The public suffers from this in two ways. Much money is wasted by needless changes of views in the progress of schemes, as, for instance, a railway company may have obtained authority for constructing a railway, which is intended to form part of a larger plan for providing facilities for communication in a certain district, but when, in a following year, it asks for powers to carry forward the line it has begun, or to make some branch in connection with it, a new committee may take a different view of the subject, and refuse it the powers it asks for, and may perhaps even practically hand over the traffic of the district to a rival company. It is notorious that in the last forty or fifty years things of this sort have repeatedly happened, with much waste of money as well as failures in securing for various districts the best arrangements that might have been made for giving them the advantage of railway communication. Perhaps still more injury has been done, and a larger amount of public money has been wasted, by the existing system of private bill legislation in another way. It is well known that the sum of money which, during the present reign, has been expended in fighting railway bills and other bills for public works of various kinds before parliamentary committees, is enormous. The loss must, in some shape or other, fall upon the public, which is also injured by the demoralising effects of so much costly litigation and of contests which, from the extreme uncertainty of their results, and the very large pecuniary interests at stake, are apt to become of a gambling character. This costly litigation is greatly increased by the uncertainty which now prevails as to whether the views adopted by Parliament in one session will be adhered to in another. Its being known that if a defeated project is again brought forward in a new session it will be referred to a different committee from that which had rejected it, encourages the promoters to make a fresh attempt to carry their point. Thus it happens that what is substantially the same question is sometimes brought before Parliament more than once, and I believe occasionally even more than twice or thrice.

These considerations, so long ago as when I was still a member of the House of Commons, led me to form a strong opinion, to which I still adhere, that a much larger and more complete change in the system of private legislation than has yet been attempted, is required. Such a change might, I believe, be best accomplished by forming a permanent body of a quasi judicial character to deal with the subjects on which private Acts of Parliament are required. All applications for such powers as are conferred by these Acts might be considered in the first instance by a body of this kind, and their decisions, in the form of "provisional orders," might afterwards be submitted for the approval of Parliament. To a certain extent this arrangement is already in existence. On the application of the parties concerned, "provisional orders" are submitted by the government for the approval of Parliament, and are now in many cases substituted with great advantage, and, with a very large saving of expense, for the private Acts formerly required to give the necessary authority for various local arrangements. But, though much good has been done by withdrawing from Parliament the original consideration of a certain class of applications for special powers, and leaving to it only the duty of confirming, or of refusing to confirm, provisional orders prepared by a department of the government, this mode of proceeding would require to be greatly modified if it were extended to the more important and often-contested applications for parliamentary powers, such, for instance, as those in which authority is sought for the construction of railways or canals. If the first consideration of projects of this kind, together with what in general would be the virtual decision upon them, is to be entrusted to any authority outside of Parliament, it ought to be to some strong and independent tribunal.

On this point the result of an attempt made by Sir R. Peel to improve the system of railway legislation is instructive. From a sense of the unsatisfactory manner in which this business was done by parliamentary committees with regard to railway schemes, he obtained in 1844 the sanction of Parliament for an arrangement by which it was provided that railway bills should be submitted to a preliminary inquiry by committees of the Board of Trade. For the performance of this duty that department was to have the assistance of a certain number of persons conversant with railway business, and Sir R. Peel meant that its reports on projected railways should serve to guide parliamentary committees in deciding on the bills brought before them. This scheme broke down, because the reports of the Board of Trade on rival railway projects failed to command the confidence of the public, and soon came to have little or no attention paid to them by parliamentary committees. There is no difficulty in understanding why this happened. The committees of the Board of Trade were not strong enough for the difficult task imposed upon them, and it was still more fatal to their authority than their want of strength, that they conducted their inquiries in private by hearing what rival projectors had to say in favour of their schemes, without the presence of their opponents. These faults, and the disapproval with which some of the reports were justly received, naturally led to doubts being generally entertained, not only as to the good judgment, but as to the fairness, of the decisions of these committees. But, though Sir R. Peel's scheme was thus unsuccessful, I believe it to have been sound in principle, and the faults which caused its failure are of such a kind as to admit of easy correction. There certainly would be no difficulty in constituting a tribunal, more competent from knowledge and experience than average select committees of either House of Parliament, to consider and decide on contested bills for the construction of railways, and for the other purposes which are answered by private Acts of Parliament. Nor is there any reason why such a properly constituted tribunal should not hear counsel and witnesses for and against proposed bills in the same public manner as committees. Fees not higher than those now paid on the passing of private Acts of Parliament would probably produce an income large enough to pay suitable salaries to a sufficient number of able men to constitute the proposed tribunal. Arrangements might easily be made for distributing its members into separate committees, which might sit at the same time in this manner, and also during as large a part of the year as the courts of law, so that no very formidable number of persons would be required to do the work of the tribunal.

By devolving to a body of this kind the chief labour of dealing with applications for private bills, Parliament would obtain great relief, and, at the same time, would give up no real authority which it now exercises. That authority, under the present system, is practically limited to its entrusting to a small number of its members the consideration of the important questions submitted to select committees on private bills, the House itself not interfering with their decisions except in the very rare cases where there are strong reasons for believing that a wrong conclusion has been come to; in such cases either House is occasionally asked to send the question back for re-consideration, either by the same, or by a fresh committee. As it is proposed that the decisions of the tribunal should be submitted to both Houses in the form of provisional orders requiring their confirmation, the existing power of calling for the re-consideration of any decision, which there may be strong grounds for believing to be wrong, would not be interfered with. The only difference would be that the original inquiry would be entrusted to a tribunal of experienced men selected for their fitness for the special duty assigned to them, instead of to a small number of peers or of members of the House of Commons, chosen in general, rather because their services are available amidst the many demands on the time of all members of the legislature, than on account of their having any peculiar qualifications for the work imposed upon them.*

I fear this explanation of the means by which Parliament might, as I believe, be relieved from labour for which it is unfit, while an important part of its work would be more efficiently performed, will be considered both tedious and somewhat irrelevant to the subject of this essay, but I have had what I think sufficient reasons for entering into it. I am convinced that it affords just ground for complaint to Ireland that private bills relating to that country have to be considered at Westminster instead of in Dublin; but I also believe this to be the only matter on

---

* Since these sentences were written my attention has been called to the debate in February 1885 on Mr. Craig Sellar's bill for altering the present system of private legislation. I was not aware that such a bill had been proposed and rejected, but, though it was rejected, I am glad to see that the existing state of things had no defenders, and that Mr. Craig Sellar was able to bring forward very strong arguments, supported by high authorities, for the change he proposed, which, in principle, was the same with that which I have suggested. The two proposals, however, differ in some important particulars, and it appears to me that Mr. Craig Sellar would have retained more of the formalities now required in passing private bills than would have been of real use under his suggested arrangement, while they would have materially diminished the benefit it would have conferred on the applicants for parliamentary powers.

which the Imperial Parliament retains in its own hands powers which ought rather to be made over to an Irish authority. This being the case, it was most important for my argument to show that the remedy for this grievance ought to be sought, not in the creation of an Irish Parliament, but in a different direction. An Irish Parliament would not be more fit than the Imperial Parliament is found to be for the duty of dealing with applications for those powers which are conferred by private Acts of Parliament. In Ireland, as in this country, applications of this kind ought, in the first instance, to be dealt with by an authority of a quasi judicial character, and there would not only be no reason for objecting to the establishment of such a tribunal in Dublin, but very strong reasons for doing so. It would not in the slightest degree impair the unity of the Imperial legislature and government, and it would be a gain, both in œconomy and convenience, to all who seek for parliamentary powers in Ireland to have their applications considered in that country.*

* A question would arise (if it were proposed to adopt the general scheme for withdrawing the first consideration of private bills from Parliament) whether there ought not to be a separate tribunal for this duty for Scotland as well as for Ireland? In

In declaring a strong opinion against the surrender by Parliament of any of its authority over Ireland to a new representative body in that country, I am far from intending to express approval of the manner in which the government of that part of the United Kingdom is now, and has long been, conducted. On the contrary, I am convinced that, both before and since the Union, Ireland has been greatly injured by the evil influence that English party politics have exercised in the management of its affairs. In the preceding pages I have endeavoured to point out some of the instances in which, from the passing of the Act of Union up to the present time, party interests and party spirit on this side of the Irish Channel have prevented the timely adoption of much-needed measures of improvement on the other. There would be little difficulty in producing further evidence to the same effect, or in showing that this unfortunate state of things did not begin

some respects this would be useful; but, on the other hand, the interests of railway companies in England and in Scotland are so closely interwoven with each other that inconvenience would arise from having railway bills for the two divisions of Great Britain considered by different authorities. The question, however, is so entirely foreign to the subject of this essay that there is no occasion for discussing it here.

with the legislative union between Great Britain
and Ireland; but that, before that measure was
adopted, Ireland suffered perhaps even more from
the cause I have referred to than it did afterwards,
until about twenty years ago. Within that time
the evil has been greatly aggravated; though
party spirit, and the endeavours of parties to use
Irish questions for party purposes, had been at the
bottom of most of the mistakes committed in the
administration of Irish affairs for a very long time,
this abuse had never previously reached to nearly
the same height that it has done since Mr.
Gladstone began his attack on the Conservative
Administration of 1868 on Irish grounds. The
opening of that attack was the beginning of a time
in which, far more than previously, we find the
strongest reasons for believing that Irish questions
of supreme importance have been dealt with not
under the guidance of an earnest desire for the
true welfare of the Irish people, and of a sound
judgment as to the best means of promoting it,
but rather of a hope that these questions might be
used successfully to gain votes in the House of
Commons for one or other of the great parties in
the State. For the reasons I have given above, I

consider Mr. Gladstone to have been by far the greatest culprit in this matter; but still his opponents cannot, I hold, be absolved from a considerable share of blame with regard to it. Much responsibility rests with them for their conduct, more especially as to the Church question, as to the legislation respecting land, and above all as to the changes which have been made in the representative system by which a predominance, or rather almost a monopoly, of political power has been given to a part of the Irish people, who, from their want of knowledge, and from their being so easily led to follow blindly the very worst advisers, are peculiarly unfit for its exercise. Passing by, however, as of little consequence, the question as to what degree of blame may justly be imputed to different parties and to different statesmen, what demands our most serious attention is the fact which must, I think, be almost universally admitted, that Ireland has been profoundly demoralised by all that has happened in the years I have been speaking of. So great is this demoralisation, and the state of the country is now so deplorable, that it is difficult to resist a feeling of despair as to the possibility of its being raised from this condition to one of prosperity and welfare of the people.

Two things are absolutely necessary in order to bring about such a change for the better; first, that the law, whatever it may be, should be firmly and effectually enforced; and secondly, that some arrangement should be adopted in order that the amendments which may be required in the law may be made more wisely than heretofore, and not at the dictates of ignorant clamour, or with a view to party interests. Of these two requisites for the amelioration of Ireland, the first is the most important. It has been often and truly said that the general poverty of the population is at the bottom of Irish discontent, and that, if the people were better off, there would not be so much disaffection. And the real reason why the country is so poor has also been often pointed out; it is, simply, that enterprise and industry have not been encouraged by security. No nation can hope to rise to wealth and prosperity except by industry and enterprise, which cannot flourish if those who devote their labour or money to the work of production have not complete security that they will be allowed to enjoy the fruits of their exertions.

This complete security has never been enjoyed in Ireland; not only has agriculture been kept down for a long series of years by faults in the law which have affected the cultivators of the soil, and by agrarian disturbances, which have more or less checked efforts to improve on the part of landowners, but, in other branches of industry also, the want of security has been felt, and has produced its natural result of discouraging exertion. It is well known that in no small number of cases promising industrial enterprises have failed in consequence of the losses suffered by their promoters from violence, and the spirit of lawless combination among those whom they employed. This evil is one of long standing. If I am not mistaken, about half a century ago the business of building and repairing ships in the port of Dublin was beginning to rise into considerable importance, when it was driven away by conduct on the part of the working shipwrights, which was at the time condemned by Mr. O'Connell (greatly to his credit), in language of just severity. The same spirit has up to this day continually shown itself among Irish labourers, and it is the insecurity thus produced, not a deficiency of natural resources in the country,—which

have, on the contrary, been shown by Sir R. Kane to
be abundant,—nor yet a want of capital,—of which
plenty would flow in if it could be safely invested,
—which has prevented any extensive demand for
labour in other occupations besides agriculture from
springing up in Ireland. The absence of proper
firmness and energy on the part of the executive
government can alone account for the long continuance of that lawlessness which has thus kept
Ireland poor, and the majority of its population in
perhaps the lowest state of any people claiming
to be civilized. Those in whose hands authority
has been successively placed cannot escape blame
for its not having been more vigorously and more
wisely used for maintaining order and security,
but though they may all have been more or less in
fault in this respect, much allowance must be made
for the circumstances in which they have been
placed. Sir R. Peel, in a speech to which I have
already referred, attributes the weakness of the
Irish government for some years before the passing
of the Roman Catholic Relief Bill to the divided
state of the administration on this question, and
since it was settled a similar effect has been produced by causes of a like kind, by the fear of

different administrations to deal resolutely with some of the grievances of Ireland, and by the use which has too often been made of Irish questions by the Opposition, whether of one party or the other, in order to embarrass the minister of the day.

Though the want of due efficiency in the executive government has, I think, done more harm to Ireland than errors and omissions in legislation, still I believe that, even before the errors of passing the Land Acts of 1870, 1881, and 1887 were committed, the failure of Parliament in the discharge of its duty of making laws for Ireland has greatly contributed to impede its improvement. To explain the grounds of this opinion would, however, require a longer statement than I think would be expedient for me to make; I will venture, therefore, to assume that a wiser and firmer exercise of the power of legislation, as well as of the executive authority, is needed by Ireland. But in the present state of the House of Commons, there is little room to hope that either of these requisites for relieving that country from the evils under which it labours can be obtained. A very large majority of the Irish members do not disguise the fact that

their great object is to make it impossible to
govern Ireland by the Imperial Parliament. And
their position affords them great advantages, if not
for accomplishing this object, at all events for
throwing difficulties in the way of the government,
not only in carrying on its parliamentary business,
but also in the performance of its executive duties.
Among other ways of doing this a practice has
been introduced of insinuating odious and utterly
unfounded charges against Irish public servants of
all ranks, from Cabinet ministers and judges to
policemen, under the guise of questions addressed
to the members of the government in the House
of Commons. Much skill is shown in putting
these questions in such a manner as to cause as
much inconvenience and annoyance as possible
without exposing those who ask them to serious
responsibility. The necessity of being constantly
prepared to meet misrepresentations made in this
mischievous manner is a serious inconvenience to
the government, and this practice of asking
questions of its members is not one of the least
effective modes by which the Irish members are
able to abuse their position in order to impede its
action.

The efforts made by those who call themselves Nationalists to embarrass the government by this and by other means would be of less consequence were it not that they receive, at least, tacit encouragement from a powerful party in this country, which leans on their support in the House of Commons. The leaders of that party have shown that they do not consider it inconsistent with their duty to abstain from any public and hearty condemnation of those who in Ireland are guilty of atrocious outrages, or what is almost worse, of using language which is sure to incite the ignorant peasants to these crimes. Nor is it only tacit support which the promoters of disorder in Ireland meet with from their English allies; it is well known what reckless and unsupported imputations have been made against the police and others who are there charged with the arduous duty of enforcing the law. With regard to the second requisite for the improvement of Ireland, the passing of well-considered and wise measures for the amendment of the law, the prospect is equally discouraging. The machinery of obstruction, which experience shows to be so formidable, will again be brought into play, and though we are assured that Her Majesty's ministers intend to propose some very strong means for putting down such attempts, it is most doubtful whether any regulations that can be adopted by the House of Commons can possibly defeat obstruction without also preventing useful discussion, so long as more than eighty Irish members, instead of wishing to assist in passing useful legislation for their country, only desire to make it plain that it cannot be governed by the Imperial Parliament and the ministers of the Crown. But it would be a great evil to impede free and fair discussion on Irish subjects, since it is greatly needed to enlighten both the Legislature and the public. We cannot disguise from ourselves that especially in the House of Commons there is a great deficiency of knowledge as to the real wants of Ireland, and what is worse, a strong disposition to listen with favour to very crude and ill-considered schemes for its improvement, and to bring pressure to bear upon the government in their support. What took place in the last Session with regard to the Land Bill affords convincing proof of the danger there is from this cause.

The facts to which I have called attention seem to me to force upon us the very grave question whether the rescue of Ireland from the evils to which it is now a prey can be looked for by any course short of suspending for a time the operation of representative government in that part of the United Kingdom, and entrusting its administration to some authority raised above party influences? I know well that no proposal for adopting so extreme a remedy for even such difficulties and dangers as those now pressing on the nation, would at present be listened to; but I believe, nevertheless, that it is what, sooner or later, we shall have to come to. It is, therefore, desirable that the idea should now be suggested, so that if, as I anticipate, the necessity for such action should arise, it may not come upon the public entirely by surprise, but that men's minds may have been in some degree prepared to consider it. That the nation may be driven, however reluctantly, to deal, in the manner I have spoken of, with the difficulties of its present position, will not appear impossible or even very unlikely to those who carefully consider what those difficulties are. So long as the great majority of the Irish

representatives continue, with the countenance of
a strong party among English and Scotch members,
to use their position in the House of Commons, in
order to thwart the action of the Imperial Parliament and Government, recent experience too
clearly proves that we cannot look either for such
legislation as is really wanted for Ireland, or for
what Lord Salisbury has truly said is still more
necessary for its welfare—a firm and impartial
exercise of the executive authority and administration of the law during a considerable time. And
while these indispensable requisites for the improvement of Ireland are unattainable under its
present system of government, Great Britain,
as well as Ireland, is suffering from the manner
in which the Irish members of the House of
Commons have systematically endeavoured to
prevent the existence of any stable administration,
by availing themselves of the party divisions in
this country, and throwing their weight alternately
into the scale of one party or the other. These
evils are fast becoming, perhaps it would be more
correct to say are already become, unbearable, and
it is difficult to guess how soon the country may
be placed under a clear and immediate necessity of

choosing between surrender to the Home Rule party or of adopting some effectual means for depriving it of the power it abuses.

When I see that there are daily more evident signs that an overwhelming majority among men of judgment and political knowledge are now fully convinced that surrender to the Home Rule party means bringing the miseries of anarchy and civil war upon Ireland, with disgrace and ruin to this great nation, I cannot believe that it will ever be agreed to. The more the subject is discussed, the better it will be understood that such a surrender would involve a shameful abandonment of a very large number of faithful and loyal subjects of the Queen to the power of men from whom they cannot expect either justice or mercy, and that it would also speedily lead to the disruption of the British Empire, unless this catastrophe should be averted by civil war.

If, seeing this to be true, the nation should before long become convinced that the present struggle must not be allowed to go on, and that therefore it is necessary to make a complete change in the system of Irish government, it is satisfactory to know that there would be no real difficulty in

discovering means by which such a change might
be accomplished. Various schemes for this purpose might be suggested, and, without pretending
to be able to form a judgment in favour of any,
I may venture to give a slight sketch of one which
has occurred to me as possible. An Act of Parliament might be passed suspending for ten years
the right of Ireland to be represented in Parliament, and entrusting its government during that
time to a Lord Lieutenant to be named in the Act.
The Lord Lieutenant so appointed not to be liable
to removal during that time, except by the Crown,
in compliance with an address from both Houses
of Parliament. The Lord Lieutenant to have full
power to carry on the executive government
according to his own judgment, and to be solely responsible for his acts, but to report all his measures
to Her Majesty's ministers, and to keep them fully
informed as to his views and intentions, so as to
enable them to call his attention to whatever
observations they might consider to be required.
The Lord Lieutenant in Council to be empowered
to make from time to time such orders, having the
force of laws, as he may think fit, but before
finally passing these orders, drafts of them pre-

pared by a committee of the Lord Lieutenant's Privy Council to be published, not less than a month beforehand, in "The Dublin Gazette," except in cases of great emergency, when they might be made at once. In order to assist the Lord Lieutenant in the work of legislation, additional members of various opinions to be added to his Privy Council. From this enlarged Privy Council the Lord Lieutenant to nominate, as occasion might arise, committees to consider such subjects as he might refer to them, and when legislation was found to be necessary they should prepare drafts of the orders in Council they might think it proper to recommend, with reports explaining the reasons for their proposals. When these reports and draft orders met with the general approval of the Lord Lieutenant, they should be published in "The Dublin Gazette" before being finally considered by him in Council, except in cases in which he might judge it to be inconvenient for some special reason to take this course. On each occasion of a meeting of the Privy Council being called, the Lord Lieutenant to decide what members should be summoned, having full discretion to summon a larger or a smaller number

of councillors according to circumstances, and to
select those whose services he considers most
likely to be useful in the business to be transacted.
When the report of a committee recommending legislation, together with a draft Order, is
brought before the Lord Lieutenant in Council, it
should be his duty to decide, after hearing the
opinion of the councillors present, whether the
Order should be passed, with or without amendments, or should be referred again to a committee
for further consideration. All Orders made by the
Lord Lieutenant in Council to be communicated
to Her Majesty's ministers and to Parliament, but
not to require to be confirmed by either.

An annual sum, equal to the average expenditure
for the public service in Ireland during the last
three or four years, should be placed by Parliament
at the disposal of the Lord Lieutenant, who
should be entrusted with unfettered discretion in
applying this money for Irish purposes, but subject
to an obligation to supply regular statements of
the manner in which it had been spent, in order
that the account might be properly audited, and
also laid before Parliament. If the Lord Lieutenant should be of opinion that a grant or loan

ought to be made from the Imperial Treasury for some important Irish purpose, he should be entitled to recommend to Her Majesty's ministers that they should apply to Parliament for the required assistance, and they should decide according to their own judgment whether such an application should be made or not.

This very slight sketch of a mode of making temporary provision for the government of Ireland during the present crisis must not be understood as describing a scheme to which I have been able to give the thought and study, without which I should not even dream of proposing any measure on a subject of such extreme importance. What I have attempted has only been to show that it is, at all events, not impossible that arrangements might be made by which the government of Ireland might for a time be carried on in such a manner as to be exempt from the pernicious influence of party spirit, and of party contests. I do not doubt that better ways of accomplishing this object than that which has occurred to me are to be found; but I feel a strong conviction that it is one it is absolutely necessary to attain, by some means or other, if Ireland is to be rescued from its miseries. In the preceding pages, I have endeavoured to prove (and I believe on evidence that cannot be contradicted) that these miseries are the result of mistakes made both in legislation and in administration, which have been mainly caused by the conflict of political parties in this country, and by the greater concern which statesmen on all sides have shown for their party than for the national interest. This evil in the last few years has been so intensified that it seems impossible that it should be got rid of, except by entrusting the powers of government to some authority strong enough to disregard all party influence, and all considerations as to what is popular, in order to adopt measures calculated to promote the real and permanent welfare of all classes of the Irish people, instead of merely gratifying the mistaken wishes of some. The arrangement, of which I have given a sketch, aims at doing this by placing <u>almost unchecked authority</u> for a limited time in the hands of a single person, adopting in this the principle acted upon in ancient days by the great Roman people, whose resource, in times of extreme peril to the Republic, was to appoint a Dictator. The dangers against which the Romans thus provided were generally of a temporary character, and the power granted to the Dictator was limited in duration accordingly; in Ireland the evils to be contended with are of long standing, and can only be cured by persevering and judicious treatment steadily adhered to for a considerable time; the authority, therefore, to which the difficult task of dealing with them is entrusted must be one not restricted to a very short, but rather looking forward to a somewhat prolonged existence. For this reason I have suggested that a Lord Lieutenant, armed with extraordinary powers, should be appointed for ten years. But I have also proposed that the same security should be taken against his misuse of his authority as that which is now given by the law against the misconduct of judges, and that the Lord Lieutenant, like a judge, should be removable by the Crown, in compliance with an address from the two Houses of Parliament. I have further suggested a method by which the Lord Lieutenant would be enabled to avail himself of the aid of the ablest men he could find in considering his measures, while the responsibility for deciding upon them would rest solely with himself. What I have now written will, I hope, be sufficient to give a general idea of the sort of government I should wish to see established in Ireland as a temporary arrangement; it would be out of place here to enter into further details as to the manner in which this idea might be carried into effect.

Before I conclude this essay I must add that I have purposely omitted from it any reference to various matters of importance which would require to be considered in settling what measures it would be expedient to adopt in order to bring about an improvement in the condition of Ireland. For instance, a very important question will arise as to whether any, and, if so, what public works ought to be undertaken there at the cost of the State in order to encourage industrial enterprise. This, and one or two other questions of the same character, would be considered with less advantage at present than they may be hereafter, when it shall have been determined whether any great change shall, or shall not, be made for a time in the system on which the executive government of Ireland, and the work of legislating for it, are now carried on. This is the great question which ought first to be considered, and, till it has been so, it would, in my opinion, be premature to enter upon any others except such as do not admit of postponement. On that great preliminary question I cannot too strongly once more express my conviction that, in order to avert the wreck of the nation, it is absolutely necessary that some means or other should be found for securing to Ireland during the present crisis a wiser and more stable administration of its affairs than can be looked for under its existing institutions, so long as the majority of its population continue to be so completely, as at present, under the dominion of excited feelings and of mistaken ideas as to what is for their real good. For this purpose I believe that some temporary measure, not less strong than that which I have described, is indispensable; but I also believe that, if some such authority as I have contemplated should be created, and be wisely and firmly used, there is no reason whatever why a great change for the better should not be accomplished in no great number of years in the social condition of this unhappy part of Her Majesty's dominions, and that a reasonable hope may be entertained that then a prosperous Irish people might send their representatives to take their share, with those of their fellow-subjects in England and in Scotland, in exercising the power of an Imperial Parlinment for the benefit of the whole British Empire.

Dec. 19*th*, 1887.

NOTES.

NOTE A.

OBSERVATIONS on the IRISH COERCION ACT of 1881, from an Article on Ireland in the "Nineteenth Century Review" for June 1882, p. 1000.

"The Act, commonly called the 'Coercion Act,' invested the Lord Lieutenant with the power of arresting and detaining any person declared by his warrant to be reasonably suspected of having been guilty as principal or accessory of certain offences in a proclaimed district. This last Act was that on which Her Majesty's ministers mainly relied for the restoration of order in Ireland. There is a very important difference between this Act and the Acts which Parliament has from time to time passed for the suspension of the Habeas Corpus

Act, either in Ireland or in this part of the United Kingdom.

"The suspension of the Habeas Corpus Act has generally been had recourse to as a preventive measure to enable the servants of the Crown to disorganise treasonable or seditious conspiracies by seizing and detaining the leaders in custody, and thus averting, or more promptly quelling, resistance to the authority of the law.* For this purpose the power has often been found most useful, but it has generally been used only against a small number of persons, and not to punish them, but to deprive them for a time of the power of carrying on seditious practices. The object has been to prevent treasonable acts from being committed, not to punish them when done. The recent Act, on the contrary, gives the Lord Lieutenant the power of issuing a warrant against any person who is 'reasonably suspected of *having been* guilty as principal or accessory' of certain offences. Under these terms of the Act (understanding them in the sense they naturally bear) it would appear that the

---

* See, for instance, the Act of 1817, 57 Geo., III. c. 3, of which the object is distinctly stated to be the protection of the Prince Regent and the Government from treasonable practices.

Lord Lieutenant and his advisers might have the strongest grounds for believing that some man was meditating an attempt to overthrow the government by force, and yet, if it could not be truly alleged that he was reasonably suspected of having been guilty of some offence already committed, no warrant could properly be issued against him. The distinction between the old measures for suspending the Habeas Corpus Act and the new Act is, therefore, exceedingly important; it is, as I have said, that the former were strictly preventive, while the latter is penal. The Act of 1881 has been used to inflict punishment—and a very heavy punishment—on a large number of persons, not for crimes, but for being 'reasonably suspected' of *having been* participators in crimes which have been committed. I certainly would not refuse to the Lord Lieutenant the power, in the present state of Ireland, of arresting those he might have reason to believe to be concerned in seditious conspiracies as a measure of prevention; but the Whig principles, in which I was brought up, and to which I firmly adhere, lead me utterly to condemn the policy of punishing men for being suspected. It may, perhaps, be said that those who have been arrested have not been so in order to punish them, and that this is shown by the mildness of the confinement they are subject to. The answer is obvious. The Act distinctly provides for their being kept in prison, not to guard against what they might do if at large, but on account of what they are suspected to *have done already*; and their confinement, however mildly it may be enforced, is, beyond all doubt, a very severe punishment indeed. To be kept within the walls of a prison for months, as some of these men have been; to be debarred from intercourse with their families and friends, except in the presence of the officers of the prison; to be deprived of the means of pursuing their ordinary avocations, which, to some of them, may mean little less than ruin; and to be compelled to submit to this dreary and monotonous existence, not for any offence of which they are shown to have been guilty, but for being 'reasonably suspected,' is, I repeat, to be subjected to a punishment which is not merely severe, but unjust and cruel. My detestation of the conduct of many of these men cannot prevent me from regarding the course which has been taken with regard to them as unjustifiable, and calculated to increase the evils under which Ireland is labouring by giving rise most naturally to a sense of wrong in the minds of the prisoners and their friends.

"I am far from desiring that any of those who have helped to bring so much misery on Ireland should escape severe punishment for their misdeeds. On the contrary, I hold it to be one of the greatest faults of the government of Ireland in the last two years that it has failed to take effectual measures for ensuring the prompt and certain punishment of all disturbers of the peace. But my sense of justice revolts against the infliction of punishment on men who have had no opportunity of defending themselves, and have seldom even known that they were accused till their punishment has been begun, and who never, I believe, have been informed of the grounds on which they have been pronounced to be 'suspected,' with the terrible consequences to them of being declared to be so. I have not the slightest doubt that the Lord Lieutenant of Ireland has signed no single warrant without being firmly convinced that the person against whom it was directed deserved to be sent to prison. I am not less sure that the Chief Secretary, and those holding responsible offices under him, have been equally anxious that no wrong should be done. But when we are told by Mr. Forster that, up to the 22nd of April, nine hundred and eighteen persons had been arrested (and, of course, the cases of a much larger number must have required to be considered), it is obviously impossible that the decisions on all these cases can have been come to on the personal knowledge of those who are responsible for them. The Lord Lieutenant and his advisers can only have acted on the information laid before them; and who will venture to affirm that this information has never been coloured by private animosities or other improper motives, or that the persons suspected might never have been able to explain the conduct for which they have become suspected, if they had been allowed an opportunity?

"Liability to abuse is inseparable from any system under which punishment is inflicted by the mere authority of the government, without any public inquiry as to the guilt of those who are subject to it. And this mode of dealing with resistance to the law in Ireland is further to be condemned for its inefficiency. Though so large a number of persons have been sent to prison, there is no sign that their punishment has done much, if anything, towards the restoration of order, and of a disposition to obey the law among the people of Ireland. Nor is there any difficulty in understanding why the severity which has been used has failed to accomplish its object. What is obviously wanted in order to put down lawlessness in Ireland (which is the real evil to be dealt with), is to provide some means by which every breach of the law, whether great or small, and every attempt to obstruct its execution, may be made to meet with prompt and fitting punishment. Towards accomplishing this, the Coercion Act does absolutely nothing. The sending to prison of ever so large a number of persons, arbitrarily selected by the government out of a very much larger number, who are equally culpable, and are not meddled with, has no tendency to create the wholesome belief that disobedience to the law will surely be followed by punishment, which can alone establish real good order on the country. To exercise the powers of the Coercion Act so largely as to punish all opponents of the law, is,

of course, impossible. The mistake has been to
use the power of arbitrary imprisonment at all for
the purpose of punishment. This power should
have been reserved, as formerly, for the protection
of the government against any attempt to overthrow it by violence, and the punishment of
offences should have been separately dealt with.
And it required to be dealt with firmly and without delay; there was urgent need for putting an
end to the impunity with which the most atrocious outrages were daily committed. Nor can I
doubt that in spite of the difficulties to be overcome, it would have been possible to devise means
by which the punishment of these crimes, in at
least the majority of cases, might have been
secured. But, unfortunately, nothing whatever
was done in this direction, though it would surely
have been better to have adopted even the strongest
measures by which men might be brought before
some sort of tribunal to be tried for the offences
they might be charged with, than to allow them
to be shut up in prison by the simple order of the
government, without any public trial at all. The
Coercion Act I therefore hold to have been an
unwise and objectionable measure. I considered

it to be so when it was brought forward. I was convinced that it would prove, as it has done, a failure, because I could see in it no marks of sound statesmanship or of skill and judgment in framing its provisions so as to accomplish its intended object. It showed, on the contrary, signs of the same hazy and indistinct conception of the proper objects of legislation, and of its principles, which suggested the Land Acts of 1870 and 1881."

NOTE B.

ON the OBJECTIONS to EMIGRATION carried on at the Public Cost, from "The Nineteenth Century," for September 1883, pp. 18–21.

"I do not doubt that emigration may be very valuable for the relief of certain districts from what has been called a local congestion of population, but I am convinced that emigration, in order to be really useful, must be effected either by the spontaneous efforts of the emigrants, and of those who expect to benefit by their departure, or by the aid of private benevolence, and that there are insurmountable objections to a large system of emigration carried on at the public cost under the direction of the government. The government could not undertake the conveyance of emigrants to a new home without arresting, or at least very greatly checking, the voluntary exertions of those who wish in this manner to better their conditions. If free passages were given to emigrants who could not find the means of paying for them, very few, indeed, would go at their own expense. The consequence would be that, if not the whole, much the greater part of the very large sums of money, which are now applied to this purpose without any demand on the public purse, would have to be supplied from the Treasury, thus imposing a needless and unjust burthen on the tax-payers, and this burthen would be incurred to no purpose. In all probability the tide of emigration would be checked instead of being increased by the interference of the government. The State would also incur an inconvenient and dangerous responsibility, both as to the selection of emigrants and as to the mode of sending them out, and of providing for them when they reached their destination. If the most distressed families, and those least able to help themselves, were sent to the United States and to our own colonies, remonstrances it would be impossible to disregard would soon come from the governments of both. Already the sending out of only an insignificant number of paupers has led to loud complaints in the United States, and to the sending back of those who had arrived. If, on the other hand, the best labourers were selected and sent out, there would be not less loud nor less just remonstrances from the counties which would thus be deprived of their most useful hands, while left to bear the burthen of the distressed and incapable among the population. The responsibility for the emigrants after their arrival would also be very onerous. When emigrants find their way out for themselves they know that they must depend upon their own exertions; they make very great exertions accordingly, and submit to the hardships they must generally at first encounter; but if the State had sent them out, they would know that it could not leave them to starve, or to become a burthen to the places where they had been sent, and their efforts to help themselves would undoubtedly be greatly relaxed. The difficulties which would thus arise could not fail to prove exceedingly serious. Again, if emigration were carried on by the State, it would not only be impossible to prevent the abuse of giving free passages to persons able to pay for themselves, but it would also be difficult to avoid the risk of sending away too many or too few emigrants. If more were sent than real necessity required, it is obvious that the productive power of the nation would be injuriously diminished; if too few, the desired relief would not be obtained. And the fact that more might expect free passages to some place offering to them greater advantages than they enjoy in their own country, would tend powerfully to prevent them from making the efforts they might to improve their lot at home, and would thus impede the advance of the nation in wealth and prosperity. No evidence has been, or, I believe, can be, adduced that the population of Ireland is at all larger than it could well maintain if its industry were properly exerted and directed; surely, therefore, it could not be good policy to spend public money in encouraging the Irish people to try to better their condition by leaving their native land, instead of by endeavouring to develope and improve its resources.

"These were some of the reasons which in 1847 and 1848 induced the government of that day to refuse to comply with the very urgent demands that were pressed upon it to undertake the task of sending from Ireland, at the public expense, a large number of those who had been left destitute by the failure, in two or three successive seasons, of the crops of potatoes on which they had depended for subsistence. After full deliberation the Cabinet of Lord John Russell came to the conclusion that, while it was most desirable that many of the people thus reduced to grievous distress should seek elsewhere for a living, they could not safely be enabled to do so at the public expense, and that it would be wise to limit the interference of the government in the matter to the two objects of guarding against the great abuses which had occurred in the conveyance of emigrants across the Atlantic, and of affording to those who went to British colonies all the assistance in finding employment for themselves, which could be granted to them without the risk of encouraging helplessness. Measures for these purposes were adopted with the cordial and very efficient aid of the colonial governments in North America. The result of this policy was that in the six years ending 31 December 1852 the total number of Irish emigrants is stated by the Emigration Commissioners in their report for 1853 to have been 1,313,226. These were the six years in which the distress in Ireland produced by the potato blight was most severe, and in which it might have been feared that it would be most difficult for the destitute population to find the means of seeking new homes without the pecuniary aid of the State; yet, without any such aid, the above large number of emigrants, which it was generally believed at the time was quite as large as was desirable, left Ireland chiefly for North America. The whole expense incurred, with the exception of the small cost of superintendence, and a sum voted by Parliament in aid of the hospitals established in the North American colonies for the relief of the sick, was provided for without any demand on the British Treasury. By far the largest part of the expense was met by remittances made by the first emigrants to assist their friends to follow them. So early as 1849 it was believed by the Emigration

Commissioners that three-fourths of the Irish emigration was paid for in this manner, and in 1858 they state in their report that the amount returned to them by the principal mercantile houses connected with America, of the remittances of this kind made through their hands in six years, was no less than £7,520,000. There must have been much more money remitted for the assistance of emigrants by their relations through other channels, of which the Commissioners had no means of obtaining any account, and, in addition to what was received from abroad, large sums were contributed at home in aid of emigration by Irish landlords and others. I believe one Irish landlord alone, the late Lord Fitzwilliam, spent no less than £50,000 in enabling those of his tenants who were reduced to the greatest distress to emigrate.

"There was a large diminution of the number of Irish emigrants after the year 1854, when the unusual distress caused by the destruction of potatoes by the disease had been to a great degree surmounted, but still up to the present time there has been a large, though fluctuating, emigration from Ireland, and a very large proportion of its cost has been defrayed by remittances from settlers to friends they have wished to assist to join them. It appears by the papers relating to the census that have been laid before Parliament that somewhat more than two millions and a half of persons had emigrated from Ireland in the thirty years ending in 1881. A paper laid last year before the House of Commons by the Board of Trade also shows that remittances to a very large amount continue to be made by settlers in North America to their friends at home, most of these sums being meant to assist emigration. The amount remitted last year in this way to the United Kingdom was above a million and a half, and I believe that double that sum is supposed to be paid annually for emigration by money provided from private sources at home or abroad. Unfortunately, I am not aware of any accessible information as to the proportion of this large expenditure which is incurred on account of emigrants from Ireland, but I cannot doubt that both the money expended without making any demand on the Treasury for Irish emigration, and the number of emigrants so sent out, must be so considerable as to make it highly inexpedient to take any steps which might be calculated to interfere with the tide of natural and healthy emigration which is now going on upon so great a scale without cost to the State. Even the comparatively small grants in aid of emigration, hitherto made from the public purse, I consider to be of very questionable expediency, as they are calculated to check voluntary exertions. To go further, and embark in a great scheme of State emigration, would, I am persuaded, be most unwise, and prove most mischievous."

www.ingramcontent.com/pod-product-compliance
Lightning Source LLC
Chambersburg PA
CBHW031738230426
43669CB00007B/385